THE
FACTS OF LIFE

JOHN TAGLIANETTI, PHD

ISBN   978-1-966473-58-9 Ebook
ISBN   978-1-966473-57-2 Paperback

The EC Publishing LLC books may be ordered through booksellers or by contacting:

EC Publishing LLC
116 South Magnolia Ave.
Suite 3, Unit F
Ocala, FL 34471, USA
Direct Line: +1 (352) 644-6538
Fax: +1 (800) 483-1813
http://www.ecpublishingllc.com/

Ordering Information:
Quantity sales. Special discounts are available on quantity purchases by corporations, associations, and others. For details, contact the publisher at the address above.

Printed in the United States of America

TABLE OF CONTENTS

LIST OF TABLES

LIST OF FIGURES

AUTHOR'S NOTE

This short book is all about the lost opportunity of men sentenced to life in prison. For these men, the only way out is to die in prison, which I call "toe tag parole." The option of commutation is a possibility except that it rarely occurs in Pennsylvania. Why are commutations so rare? While some state legislatures constrained or eliminated parole in the 1990s, in most states the parole board still has enormous power to offer second chances to incarcerated people. But most parole boards—including for many years, Pennsylvania's and Connecticut's—have refused to do so. As the criminal justice scholars Kevin R. Reitz and Edward E. Rhine note, parole board members are risk-averse political appointees with little job security. "Members or entire boards," they write, "have been forced to resign after a single high-profile crime committed by a released prisoner." Typically, parole boards are most hostile toward those who have committed crimes of violence, often refusing to consider anything other than the offense itself during rote hearings as they relitigate the offenses that morph into decades of denials.

That is why it matters so much that the nation's parole board should begin to chart a new course. More than 50% of people in state prison are serving sentences for violent crimes. We will never end the scourge of mass incarceration if we write off this group. Because decades of research have proved that older people are rarely violent, extremely long sentences can almost never be justified on public safety grounds. And because some incarcerated people have found ways to change and thrive in conditions few of us could tolerate, the system should have pathways that recognize their efforts and reward them with paroles.

PROLOGUE

How did we end up with life without parole (LWOP) as the predominant sentence for criminal convictions used in Pennsylvania? One answer is that LWOP is the often-praised alternative to the death penalty. Life without parole, in some ways, has outcomes that are contrary to what progressive lawyers and sentencing reform advocates argue for. LWOP is no different than the death penalty in one respect, because it leaves no possibility of redemption or eventual freedom. In these cases, prisoners are incarcerated not for rehabilitation, but for retribution and vengeance. Any chance of accountability and personal transformation is made moot. Of the 23 states that do not practice the death penalty, Alaska is the only state that does not permit life without parole as a possible sentence. Among the eleven states that have abolished the death penalty since 2007, all do allow sentences for life without parole. In 1972, the Supreme Court declared that under then-existing laws "the imposition and carrying out of the death penalty... constitutes cruel and unusual punishment in violation of the Eighth and Fourteenth Amendments" (Furman v. Georgia, 408 U.S. 238). However, not enough attention has been accorded—in theory or policy—to the ways in which LWOP too constitutes cruel and unusual punishment.

CHAPTER 1

Introduction

It is a difficult fact for many to comprehend, yet it is true: The United States incarcerates people at a higher rate than any other nation in the world (Smoyer et al., 2019). Today, the U.S. criminal justice system holds 2.3 million people in 1,719 state prisons, 109 federal prisons, 1,772 juvenile correctional facilities, 3,163 local jails, and 80 Indian Country jails. In addition, there are military prisons, immigration detention facilities, civil commitment centers, state psychiatric hospitals, and prisons in the U.S. territories (Prison Policy Initiative, 2019). These numbers are large and have grown exponentially over the past three decades (Luallen & Cutler, 2017). Incarceration rates are higher than rates of release and parole, and long-term prisoners are aging-in-place. According to the Sentencing Project (2020) report, the United States now holds an estimated 40% of the world population serving life imprisonment and 83% of those serving without parole. The increase in life imprisonment sentences in the United States has fueled the exponential growth of the prison population in the United States.

A population of about 207,000 inmates are currently serving life sentences (10.9% of the entire prison population). This number exceeds the size of the *entire* prison population in 1970 of 197,000 (Nellis, 2017). By state, there are 24 states where far more people are serving life sentences than were in prison overall in 1970. In an additional nine states, the life imprisonment total is within 100 people of the 1970 prison population. Because lifers, by definition, remain in the prison system, there is a marked aging of the prison population and 30% of lifers (61,417) are 55 years old or more: triple the number in 2000. Along with the normal effects of aging, prisoners experience accelerated aging. The acceleration is due to severe trauma, poor health management, and the population's stressors. The current penal system will face increasingly high costs and challenges to prisoner care as aging continues (Maschi & Aday, 2014). Speaking to the prevalence of prejudice in our judicial system, 67% of lifers are people of color, while only 40% of the U.S. population are people of color. Ten percent of the prison population is female.

There are three primary types of lifetime sentences. First, there are life without the possibility of parole (LWOP) sentences. There are also life sentences with restrictive parole practices in certain jurisdictions. Lastly, there are virtual life sentences, which are prison sentences of such length that the prisoner has no chance of outliving them (Henry, 2012). Such a sentence may be composed of a single sentence, or multiple sentences required to be served consecutively – not in parallel. A variety of different terms and acronyms are used: life without the possibility of parole (LWOP), death in prison (DIP), death by incarceration (DBI), the other death penalty (ODP) and virtual life sentences. The terminology of "men serving life sentences" is meant to identify men who have been sentenced to LWOP, DBI, virtual life, or life in prison (Crewe, 2015). Regardless of which acronyms and descriptions are used, they all have primarily the same impact: a death sentence. The inmate will die in prison without ever finishing his sentence (Nellis, 2013).

Criminology scholars have often highlighted the negative consequences of mass incarceration, including life sentences. Children are impacted when their parents are taken away. Our democracy is threatened when 5.2% of Americans cannot vote because of a felony conviction. The prisoners themselves suffer bodily health impacts such as an increased rate of Tuberculosis and HIV (Sadiq & Parveen, 2014). Imprisonment affects mental health, too. Examples include victimization, hypervigilance, social withdrawal, depression, and a diminished sense of self (Singer, 2012). Due to the effects of experiences encountered while serving life sentences, the older men appear to be 15 years older than their actual chronological age in mental health and physical health (Hayes et al., 2012). This severe and accelerated aging occurs due to stress, adversity, general poor health, and other stressors (Maschi & Aday, 2010).

While a handful of studies have examined the incarcerated older male population, they have focused solely on mental health and relied on data collected from prison records, guards, administrators, and various other stakeholders or custodial staff, neglecting the prisoners' subjectivity (Vollm & Deming, 2017). Regrettably, positive outcomes have received little attention. One study found that those with life and long-term sentences develop coping mechanisms to adapt to the incarceration experience (MacKenzie & Goodstein, 1985). These include social, psychological, and behavioral changes among older male inmates that move their lives in a more positive direction. Those serving life sentences spend even more years incarcerated than non-lifers, and therefore have more opportunities for adaptation and adjustment (Sliva, 2015; Kazemian & Travis, 2015). For most of these inmates, significant changes may occur in their lives as they develop as human beings and as they focus on developing and exhibiting a prosocial attitude.

What are lifers' lived experiences with adjustment and adaptation? There is a cost to ignoring the potential benefits of addressing lifers' needs, as well as important ethical issues. These issues pertain to human rights and social justice (Tonry, 2011). Furthermore, these inmates can make valuable contributions and can help the development of a healthier prison climate.

As part of my work toward obtaining a Ph.D. in Psychology at Walden University (headquartered in Minneapolis, Minnesota), I did a dissertation. It explored the perspectives of older men serving life sentences in Graterford State Correctional Institution, a maximum-security prison in Eastern Pennsylvania. My goal was to obtain insight into adjustments and changes made by these men that produced a positive outcome for them. This book is a continuation of that work and is designed to bring my findings and insights to a more general readership.

Theoretical Framework

There is a theory in the fields of criminology and psychology that is called *Adaptation Theory*. (See *Glossary of Terms* in the Appendices for the definition of terms used throughout this book.) It was developed primarily by Clemmer, who coined the term *prisonization* to refer to the adoption of the folkways, mores, customs, and general culture of the inmate subculture (1940). Through prisonization, inmates come to accept several "universal factors of prisonization," including the inmate's acceptance of an inferior role, learning to adapt to the regulations and structure of the prison, and learning to become passive about one's own needs—many of which are automatically taken care of by the institution.

Taylor (1983), who expanded the Clemmer theory, asserted that all human beings are extraordinarily resilient. When faced with major threatening life events such as life in prison, humans will adapt to their environment in a way that fosters their well-being. He suggests that humans cope with threats in their lives by creating a set of positive concepts or illusions that serve to protect their psychological health. These positively slanted cognitions create space for hope, personal growth, and flexibility.

While the ability to cope in a positive way with a life of incarceration can deteriorate with aging, aspects of prison life for individuals can improve based on a long-term adaptation process (Aday, 2014). Improvement in adaptation entails coping mechanisms such as educational programs, helping other younger inmates, religiosity, artistic expression, and eventual commutation.

There is limited understanding of how older male inmates cope with incarceration and achieve positive adjustment through adaptation processes. In psychology, *adaptation* is defined as a process by which individuals or groups make necessary or desired changes—cognitive, behavioral, and affective—in response to new environmental conditions or demands as a way to meet basic needs, function within their situation, and maintain a good quality of life. The process of adaptation to imprisonment is almost always painful and, at times, creates habits of thinking and acting that can be dysfunctional (Dhami, 2015). Kazemian and Travis (2015) identified a number of correlations of adjustment to prison. They noted that learning more about how prisoners experience and cope with prison life is essential to understanding and improving inmate adjustment, and thus enhance prisons' efficiency. Outcomes remain understudied, and the findings are sometimes inconsistent.

Some components of a prison program can be beneficial through the adaptation process. For example, prisoners can benefit from educational opportunities, anger management techniques, abstinence from drugs, and prevention of alcohol abuse (Aday, 2014). However, most long-term prisoners are excluded from educational and reentry programs in the current correctional system because basic rehabilitative programs are only offered to prisoners with shorter sentences. Research has shown that older LWOPs mental and physical health needs are not being met, and there is a lack of resources to address their needs (Flatt et al., 2017). Therefore, an increased understanding of LWOPs' experiences could encourage prisons to improve access to rehabilitative programs for this population to help meet their adaptive needs.

Scarcity of Current Research on the Subject

Existing research on how those serving sentences achieve positive adjustment and adaptation during incarceration is minimal. Increasing knowledge of inmate adjustment to prison practices is a viable way to improve prisons' efficiency. Understanding this topic is relatively limited, and there are still several gaps that warrant further inquiry. Most previous research relied on stakeholder groups' perspectives other than prisoners, which neglected inmates' subjectivity. Although researchers have identified many aspects of prison adjustment, many predictors and outcomes are still understudied, while the results of existing studies have been inconsistent (Smoyer et al., 2019). Most previous research relied on stakeholder groups' perspectives rather than prisoners, thus neglecting inmates' perspectives. More specifically, Smoyer et al. (2019) reported that of 16 qualitative studies related to this subject, only two were peer-reviewed and both were decades-old.

Di Lorito et al. (2018) analyzed data collected directly from prisoners and formerly incarcerated older adults, rather than stakeholders. They identified 25 papers, of which 16 were qualitative. Only two of these concerned older adults' lived experiences, and those articles were not peer-reviewed. Thus, this population's voices and perspectives are muted, inhibiting efforts to create interventions to meet their specific needs (Haugebrook et al., 2010). As Kazemian and Travis (2015) stated, not all existing research has suggested deterioration in prisoners' adjustment over the length of time incarcerated. MacKenzie and Goodstein (1985) indicated that long-termers and lifers who have spent long years in prison develop coping mechanisms to adapt to the incarceration experience. Leigey (2010), Zamble (1992), and Zamble and Porporino (1998) all reported that prisoners employ different adaptation techniques. Inmates serving long-term sentences are characterized by attitudes and behavior designed to facilitate survival in prison.

Learning more about how older male prisoners serving life sentences adjust to and cope with prison life is essential to understanding how programs to enhance their ability to adapt can be implemented (Leigey, 2015). An increased knowledge of inmate adjustment to prison practices is a viable way to improve prisons' efficiency. Inmate adjustment to prison is also necessary concerning several essential correctional practices: explaining institutional infractions, health care utilization, and coping strategies (Goncalves, 2014).

Adaptation Mechanisms

According to Willis and Zaitlow (2015), surviving imprisonment is complicated and challenging for most who serve long sentences. LWOPs are individuals, and each man can have different adaptation mechanisms. Further, while persons serving life sentences include those sentenced to capital offenses, they also include those whose sentence length is uncertain. LWOP sentences for nonviolent crimes misuse correctional resources and discount the capacity for personal growth that results from time passage. Macchio (1994) reported that lifers experience tremendous tension at the commencement of their sentences. They attempt to neutralize stress by learning prison subcultural norms during this initial period of incarceration. As a result of this effort, they bond with the prison world and adapt a prison code of behavior. This adaptation helps them survive in the prison environment. Through a slow, cautious, and strategic process, they develop friendships with others also sentenced to life in prison. However, existing research has not accorded sufficient attention to this phenomenon of induction into the prison environment. Interestingly, most lifers reject identifying themselves simply as convicts, preferring to adopt the identity of "lifer" (Macchio, 1994, p. x).

Flanagan (1995) noted that early studies suggested that the effects of extended prison stays were predictable and negative. Prior studies reported personality deterioration, dependence on institutional life, and ever-increasing levels of prisonization: also called an oppositional inmate value system. In contrast, Flanagan stated that the changes that occur are in an unexpectedly positive direction. He suggested that scholars' thinking about long-term incarceration's effect had come full circle from the early deterioration model. Flanagan's study demonstrated that many long termers successfully adapt and adjust, but the strategies they use to do so are not easy to deduce and even more difficult to classify.

How Prison Changes People

Mackenzie and Goodstein (1985) stated that long-term confinement's adverse effects had not been demonstrated satisfactorily in any existing empirical research. They also indicated that they found no evidence of psychological deterioration over time, despite some transitional issues during the initial period of incarceration. They argued that lifers do adapt successfully to life in prison. Haney (2001) noted that how the inmate adapts to the demands of being incarcerated contributes to what he calls *prisonization*. Wormith (1984), in reviewing sociological literature, claimed the prison experience is very complex and interactive. He also suggested that researchers should not embrace the practice of using terms like *institutionalization* or *prisonization*, nor should the researchers use any single model such as importation and deprivation. Porporino and Zamble (1984) asserted the literature focusing on the prison experience is deficient in advancing an understanding of adaptation or adjustment processes and changes that occur to the long-term inmate during incarceration. Porporino and Zamble also stated that many other researchers have suggested that, while the prison experience contributes to prisoners' criminal self-identification, there is no explanation of as well as how criminal or convict identity emerges. Their study concluded that variations in individual perspectives and coping strategies affect how criminal self-identification emerges in prison.

Further, it is unclear why researchers fail to successfully adapt to the prison environment as a form of identity transformation. They also stated that further research is required to address transformation or behavioral change in the existing study and the effects of long-term incarceration. According to Porporino and Zamble (1984), the reason is that there is a variation of individual perspectives and coping strategies that affect how criminal self-identification emerges in prison.

Flanagan (1981) stated that living in prison for a prolonged period significantly affects long-term inmates. Adaptation to the prison environment occurs when prisoners adopt new behaviors, coping strategies, and attitudes. Smit et al. (2019) noted that adjustment is even more difficult when there is uncertainty about eventual release. Smit et al. suggested that lifers tend to experience homelessness due to their sentences. However, Porporino and Zamble (1984) are critical of Flanagan, stating that researchers have failed to prove that individuals change due to lengthy incarceration.

As Miszewski (2017) noted, most of the literature on LWOPs is quite dated and deals with countries outside the United States. The inmates' perspectives are also ignored in favor of other prison stakeholders' views, and negative aspects are prioritized. The report also noted that penitentiary policy has typically placed long-term prisoners at the very bottom of their priorities list. Long-term prisoners are usually excluded from educational programs, reentry programs, and basic rehabilitative programs afforded to prisoners with shorter sentences. Approximately 42% of the nearly 2 million men currently incarcerated are over age 50, and the current number of imprisoned individuals serving life sentences is 161,957 (Carson, 2016; Carson & Sabol, 2016). Though attention to the older male incarcerated population has increased somewhat, research has primarily addressed mental health and relied on data collected from stakeholders other than the inmates themselves (Kreager et al., 2017; Vollm and Deming, 2017).

Pains of Imprisonment

Most lifers face a lonely death while incarcerated, usually in their declining years when they pose a minimal threat to society. Johnson and Tabriz (2011) report that a disturbing number of them will commit suicide as their means of escape. They opined that people serving life sentences are essentially a class of living dead. They are often sentenced to lonely and untimely deaths due to traumatic stress and anxiety while incarcerated. In contrast, Zamble (1992) studied lifers for seven years and found that they did not exhibit negative adaptation in ways that would inhibit their quality of life after imprisonment or make it more challenging to cope outside. They did not sink into despair, depression, or rebellion. They improved their emotional states, health, and conduct, and, most importantly, their ability to cope with adversity. However, the study commenced with inmates very close to the beginning of their sentences, with follow-up interviews 16 months later, when the inmate is still in the adjustment period. It is an open question if Zamble's (1992) use of only recently sentenced prisoners limits the applicability of the conclusions.

There is minimal research on how those serving sentences achieve positive adjustment and adaptation during incarceration. Increasing knowledge of inmate adjustment to prison practices is a viable way to improve prisons' efficiency. Understanding this topic is relatively limited, and there are still several gaps that warrant further inquiry. According to Smoyer et al. (2019), most research has relied on data collected through the perspectives of stakeholder groups other than prisoners, which neglects the subjectivity. Smoyer et al.'s (2019) examination has shown that of the 16 qualitative studies found, only two were peer-reviewed and were decades-old.

According to Sliva (2015), researchers have identified many aspects of prison adjustment, many predictors and outcomes are still understudied, and the results of existing studies have been inconsistent. Similarly, Goncalves (2014) argued that learning more about how older male prisoners serving sentences adjust to and cope with prison life is essential to understanding how programs to enhance their ability to adapt can be implemented. Inmate adjustment to prison is also necessary to consider several vital correctional practices: explaining institutional infractions, health care utilization, and coping strategies (Goncalves, 2014).

Long-Term Experiences and Adaptation

Macchio (1994), in her ethnographic study as a former lifer in a Canadian prison, said lifers experience tremendous tension at the commencement of their sentences. The lifer neutralizes stress by learning prison subcultural norms during this initial incarceration period. They bond with the prison world and adapt a prison code of behavior. Through a slow, cautious, and strategic process, they develop friendships with others also sentenced to life in prison. However, this phenomenon of induction into the prison environment and the manifestation of a criminal or convict identity has not been supported by other research. Macchio concluded lifers reject identification as a convict and lifer as an identity prevails. Mackenzie and Goodstein (1985) also stated that the long-term adverse effects had not been demonstrated satisfactorily in any existing empirical research. They found no evidence of psychological deterioration over time. Even though there are some transitional issues during the initial period of incarceration, lifers do adapt successfully to life in prison.

Wormith (1984), in reviewing specific sociological literature, claimed the prison experience is very complex and interactive. Researchers should not embrace the practice of using terms like institutionalization or prisonization, nor should the researchers use any single model such as importation and deprivation (Dhami et al., 2007). Porporino and Zamble (1984) said there is a need to expand our understanding of adaptation to the prison environment. They felt that literature focusing on the prison experience is deficient in advancing an understanding of adaptation or adjustment processes, and change that occurs to the long-term inmate during incarceration. They also stated that researchers reference the prison experience as the catalyst contributing to a prisoners' criminal self-identification. However, they do not explain how criminal, or convict identity emerges. Moreover, they also stated that further research is required to address deficiencies in the existing study of the effects of long-term incarceration. According to Porporino and Zamble (1984), the reason is that there is a variation of individual perspectives and coping strategies that affect how criminal self-identification emerges in prison. Flanagan (1981) said adaptation to the prison environment occurs while prisoners adopt certain behaviors, coping strategies, and attitudes. However, Porporino and Zamble (1984) are critical of Flanagan, stating that researchers have failed to prove that individuals change due to lengthy incarceration. The current study will demonstrate from the point of view and descriptions of the effects of lengthy incarcerations.

Kazemian and Travis (2015) stressed the importance of including long-termers and lifers in research and policy, although numerous studies have failed to do so. Though those serving sentences spend a significant part of their lives in prison, policies and programs are rarely tailored to their needs. Miszewski (2017) has reported that the long-termers' social needs, especially the older long-timers, are different from those of the young inmates. Overall, little is known about adaptation, practical interventions, or how to measure programs' effectiveness from this population's perspective.

Clemmer (1958) noted that a primary determinant of how a prisoner becomes adapted is the length of the sentence being served. Toch (1975) suggested that adaptation to prison varies based on the prisoner's personality and other factors like the type of prison and staff perspectives. Singer (2015) stated that incarcerated men have psychological responses to the environment in which they live. The physically and emotionally aggressive atmosphere of prison requires heightened protection for the self. She argues that it is necessary to shift perceptions away from seeing these psychological adaptations in prison as disturbances and instead realize that they are unique survival achievements towards maintaining one's mind, spirit, and body in prison.

Taylor (1961) reported that the long-term prisoner responds to imprisonment physically but not psychologically because of the restrictions and deprivations of imprisonment. Pickering (1966) noted that long confinement results in damage to the personality. Flanagan (1981) contended that deterioration among long-term inmates is accepted *a priori*, both intellectually and emotionally. Goffman (1961) found that long-term imprisonment causes dependence upon the institutional regime, and prisoners lose interest in the outside world during prisonization. Carlson (2013) reported that that adaptation is essential and that conducting a qualitative inquiry on this subject enables researchers to explore, understand, and analyze the adaptation processes in depth. Herbert (2019) stated that individual participants are best placed to describe situations and feelings in their own words. Complementing Herbert's study of this current study, the research data may demonstrate how inmates can adapt in a constrained environment when applied. In addition, LWOPs can be encouraged to cultivate and influence shareholders to regard the rehabilitation of LWOPs as essential, in order to motivate correctional officials and society to instigate social change.

CHAPTER 2

Literature Review

Adaptation to the prison environment has been a matter of scholarly debate. Most such discussions have addressed the extent to which adaptation is influenced by the prison environment itself (indigenous) or by the prisoners' pre-prison character (imported experiences). Lifers are low-maintenance prisoners. They cause minor confrontations and keep to themselves. Sliva (2015) stressed that, for inmates, acceptance of the self correlates with varying levels of hope. The conceptual model that emerged indicated that long-term lifers experience imprisonment with feelings of profound loss, much like the feelings one might feel in response to losing a loved one. She describes the initial shock during which the inmate will pass through various emotional stages such as denial, anger, possibly depression, and in the end, acceptance. Inmates find a way to exercise personal choice. They find ways to forge meaning from their pain and suffering. She states that the process draws close parallels with Frankl's (1969) theory of human resilience and survival.

Similarly, Taylor (1983) expanded Nelson's theory and suggested that severe personal setbacks can recover from adversity wholly and quickly through adaptation. Adaptation involves understanding an event and its impact through a search for meaning. Taylor's study demonstrates Viktor Frankl's (1970) Logotherapy's validity and usefulness in man's search for meaning. Adjustment is the process by which individuals adopt new behaviors that facilitate their ability to cope with change. Long-termers will adjust or shift their adaptive strategies while seeking a plan until they find the one most functional for their prison environment (Taylor, 1983).

Nelson (1983) suggested that individuals serving sentences tend to come to what could be called a realistic assessment of their situation. While facing life in prison, early on, they experience a period of being unsettled. The timeframe can be months or even years. During this uncertain time, they may suffer from depression and feel suicidal. Johnson and Dobrzanska (2005) have suggested that those serving life sentences grudgingly accept that, while prison is not the life they want or desire, it is all they have, and they must adapt to survive. However, adaptive choices offer only an illusion of control. Making choices is a fundamental human need that has limited scope in institutional settings (Toch, 1998). Individuals serving life sentences typically come to a realistic assessment of the grim situation they face. Caceral (2004) suggested that many individuals serving sentences opt to make the best of the limited work opportunities and avoid trouble. While taking advantage of all education and rehabilitative programs, they eventually accept prison as their home and the other inmates as their adopted family (Johnson 2002).

Imperative for Inclusion of LWOP Inmates in Research and Policy

The research on the adaptation and adjustment of LWOPs and how they experience their imprisonment is limited. Therefore, their impact on prison administrators' and legislators' efforts to intervene and meet their needs is reduced (Haugebrook et al., 2010). Frisch (2018), who studied framing imprisonment as a catalyst for behavior modification, suggested that focusing on older inmates is essential. Older inmates are more likely to exhibit a positive change than younger offenders, who are more likely to show negative changes. The younger prisoners are generally focused on getting out of prison with little interest in any offered programs. The older prisoners sentenced to life are looking to improve themselves in the hope of one day being released from prison. Sliva (2015) examined the experiences of men who are subject to life without parole through open-ended interviews. The research incorporated four existing studies—containing interviews with 86 men serving sentences—to build a more extensive understanding of the phenomenon of adaptation and adjustment to life in prison.

Adaptation and Autonomy

How do these inmates achieve autonomy? As concluded by Zamble (1992), they must accept deprivation and the fact that they have very little control over their situation. Paulich (2004) suggested that those serving life sentences often make incarceration their own by living routines and choosing to consent to things they cannot change or avoid. Sorensen and Wrinkle (1998) noted that those serving life sentences often stay out of trouble because it would jeopardize the life they have achieved within the prison culture.

While younger prisoners are impulsive, disruptive, and usually dangerous, those serving life sentences generally mature while imprisoned, developing self-control. They also become much more thoughtful as they mature and age. Individuals serving sentences usually attempt to mentor young inmates to help them avoid making the mistakes they themselves made. Groups of inmates serving life sentences can provide a source of companionship and a productive activity through mentoring young prisoners and giving back to the next generation (Paulich, 2004). These activities belie the myth that inmates serving life terms live out their lives in a state of passivity and simply atrophy. As prison routines shape this population, they also typically develop personal habits. Even though adaptation is an ongoing and arduous process, most are not worn down, and adapt to their environment. Accordingly, they not only survive but often do so with little or no psychological damage, and most express a tremendous increase in prosocial values and attitudes and favorable psychological profiles (Wormith, 1984; Zamble, 1984; Zamble & Porporino, 1984).

Positive Adaptation Experiences

Maruna (2004) noted that most people believe it is possible to change their own lives. However, these same people do not accept the potential for change among inmates serving life sentences. As noted earlier, existing research has overlooked positive experiences for prisoners and personality adaptations among this group. Despite surviving adversity, members of this population care less about the views of society than about their own adaptation and rehabilitation processes (Herbert, 2019).

Notably, most studies included in Sliva's (2015) meta-synthesis only highlighted incarceration's negative aspects. Kazemian and Travis (2015) suggested that this oversight is noteworthy given that previous research failed to document the social, behavioral, and psychological changes that occur during long incarceration periods. Therefore, scholars have not developed a sufficient understanding of this population to facilitate effective interventions. They are also unable to measure the effectiveness of adaptation. As Willis and Zaitlow (2015) noted, prisoners adopt specific coping methods and adjusting to the pressures of life in confinement. They also must balance the risks associated with quietly standing out. A long-term prisoner who aspires to accomplish goals during incarceration might be viewed as offensive to the administration because such a prisoner is "not truly a prisoner." After all, his or her mind is free. Most correctional administrations appear to prefer that prisoners limit themselves to their functions as prisoners, doing time without attracting attention or disrupting the system. It is an environment where such seemingly effortless activities as holding onto one's identity and sanity take on a significance of paramount importance (Willis & Zaitlow, 2015).

Crewe et al. (2017) examined how those serving sentences adapted over time to their circumstances. They discussed experiences through the subsequent stages of sentences, significantly how the prisoners changed concerning time management, shifting conceptions of control, making their sentence constructive, and, most importantly, moving from reactive to productive adjustments in behavior. In his address at the Center for Criminology (Crewe, 2016), he outlined the shift from a reactive agency to a productive agency at last sentences. He found that this was accomplished in four transitional stages:

- Adapting to the sentence.
- Achieving an accurate perception of time.
- Practicing control and self-control.
- Finally coming to terms with the offense.

In the end, they finally achieve a purpose. They were able to view education and other ways of betterment to give something back. This provides a sense of doing something positive to atone for the harm they had caused. He noted that too little attention has been accorded to the life experiences and effects of adjustment and adaptation associated with sentences.

Motivations for Adaptation

Rocque et al. (2016) investigated the causes of desistance from crime and reported positive behavior changes among male inmates over time. They also questioned whether these adjustments could predict actual behavior. Rocque et al. (2016) suggested that their study demonstrates that future qualitative studies should thoroughly examine determinants of adaptation. Siennick and Osgood (2008) studied people who become attached to conventional roles. They found that those who adapt will be reluctant to jeopardize these roles by offending. They will be further restrained from crime by the sense of obligation and responsibility that accompanies these roles. Laub and Sampson (2003) showed that holding a role reduces crime depending on the strength and quality of the social bonds engendered by the position.

According to Jarman (2017), most criminologists have developed only conceptual accounts of change in the criminal agency. Most importantly, researchers have not used these tools to consider adaptation or change among prisoners with long sentences. This study expanded the understanding of the known styles of adaptation and clarified some conclusions about the kinds of conditions that can support prisoner change. One example offered was that the prison's social life is the main feature of the corrective agency and the development of practices that demonstrated a dedication to 'positive' norms and self-betterment to peers. These can be seen as 'desistance signals' (see Maruna, 2012), and they reinforced changed identity at the cost of subcultural credibility.

Frisch (2018) investigated the extent to which prison serves as a positive or negative influence in a criminal career. Behavior before and after confinement, including the process of adaptation in criminal behavior, was examined. The study also looked at timing, age-graded transitions, and how prison serves as a positive or negative influence. Lattimore et al. (2018) conducted interviews with 174 male prisoners of various ethnicities in Great Britain regarding how they experienced prison. The authors discussed the need for more studies focusing on the dynamic process of desisting from criminal thought and activity. They emphasized the working self and individuals' self-description of committing to the active illegal self until they realized that the costs outweighed the benefits.

Prison and Identity Change

Lattimore et al. (2018) found that it was not until the criminal identity weakens that there is a chance for positive identity change. The perceived sense of a future or of possible self as a non-offender—coupled with the fear that one faces a bleak and highly undesirable future—motivates inmates to break from crime without change. Paternoster et al. (2016) found that offenders who desist undergo an identity transformation when they realize that they need to adapt and change to avoid the hopelessness associated with dying in prison. However, Paternoster et al. (2016) suggested that further research is required to substantiate that lack of social identity and agency, caused by hopelessness among those with life sentences. Leban et al. (2015) studied 40 inmates in a maximum-security prison. They found that older inmates were less prone to criminality due to their long experience with incarceration and by achieving a diverse repertoire of perspectives about their adaptation to newly acquired larger life goals. The researchers stated that their findings shed light on effective coping strategies and psychological factors that require further critical attention.

Crank (2010) stated that many studies have focused on the relationship between prison adjustment and inmate age and found that the more experience prisoners have with incarceration, the less difficulty they have in coping with younger prisoners. Previous research stated that experienced inmates could adjust to prison life with less anxiety, as older inmates develop and learn systems for dealing physically and mentally with incarceration (Shover, 1985). Jarrett (2018) stated that prisonization could lead to post-incarceration syndrome upon release and suggested that if prisoners are hardened in the beginning stages of incarceration, they are likely to become even more challenging, colder, and more distrustful while incarcerated. Meijers et al. (2017) noted that traits such as self-discipline, ambition, and orderliness deteriorate during incarceration due to the harsh environment. Crewe (2015) challenged this pessimistic outlook, suggesting that some prisoners try to make a good impression and reflect a positive personality adjustment to prison life. The argument is proffered that criminals can be equally pro-socially motivated just as the general population's members. However, as Jarrett (2018) stated, there is a dearth of existing research on positive adaptation and coping. As awareness regarding the malleability of personality grows, it will lead to further studies about how the prison environment can shape the inmates' character in a positive way. Flanagan (1982) stated that the foundations that created their deterioration were from earlier research. He claimed that his rigorous study indicated that no systematic or predictable long-term incarceration effects exist.

Age and Adaptation

Shover (1985) noted that as they have aged, older inmates felt time passed more quickly than it did when they were young. Older inmates often considered time was being wasted and valued their remaining years. Older inmates find prison challenging because of their changed perception of time (Crank, 2015). Overall, older inmates are more experienced and have less difficulty coping with imprisonment than younger inmates. Crank (2015) suggested that recently incarcerated older inmates adjust with less stress because they develop and learn systems and means to adapt and cope physically and mentally throughout the incarceration experience. Her finding echoes Shover (1985): inmates grow tired of being hardened and weary of the possibility of re-arrest and a lengthy prison sentence.

The relationship between age and the perceived difficulty of prison life can explain older prisoners' positive adaptation. Older LWOP inmates are affected by the aging process and encounter many medical conditions that make them more likely to suffer DBI. According to Cornelius et al. (2017), the relationship between age and crime is the most vital and tested element studied in criminology. According to Farrington (1986), criminality increases in adolescence, peaking at age 17 and decreases as the individual ages. He notes that involvement and belief that prison norms are essential and that a violation of these norms will lead to consequences.

In contrast, Santos (2003) suggested that the long-term prisoner grows accustomed to prison, and it no longer feels like a prison to them. Prison becomes a way of life: inmates' lives are routine and predictable, even though they are harshly restricted and sometimes inhumane. Shover (1985) also noted that even though some inmates perceive themselves as adapting well to incarceration and prison life, the correctional officers and prison officials may regard the same inmates as adapting poorly. Therefore, it is essential to examine inmate perceptions of the difficulty or incarceration to understand the inmates' adjustment to prison life fully.

Adjustment, Adaptation, and Acceptance

According to Jarrett (2018), there is little hope for adjustment. He stated that if the prisoner is hardened initially, he will become even more demanding and colder by imprisonment, and reintegration will become more complex, if not impossible. Dhami et al. (2007) addressed similar issues regarding adaptation and prison outcomes. They focused on the longevity of imprisonment and life quality before prison to examine both influences' relative effect. The indigenous approach, or deprivation model, addresses pains or deprivations; at the same time, prison is the primary catalyst for inmates' responses to imprisonment.

According to the importation approach, prison outcomes are influenced by the prisoners' pre-prison character and history, including previous imprisonment, drug use, relationships, employment, and education. Using survey results, Camp et al. (2003) found that features of inmates' lives before imprisonment may combine to affect their adaptation to captivity. Concerning the possibility of synthesizing the validity of the indigenous and importation approaches in a single study, Camp et al. (2003) stated just such an effect. They found that the importation approach was a better predictor of prison violations than the indigenous method. However, they discounted several importation approaches (e.g., education, employment, drug use, mental illness, and prior offenses) and suggested that these found that other factors were not significant predictors. On the other hand, as noted, the traditional theories are incomplete. They ignore contact with the outside world during imprisonment, which may influence the support of the importation approach.

For example, former inmates may have been exposed to similar rules and ways of life in other contexts, and therefore adapt to prison life quality and deprivation while incarcerated with ease (May et al., 2008).

Crank (2010) cited very little existing research had done so. More recent qualitative studies on inmate perceptions have been based on small samples. Crank began her research with old literature (Beccaria, 1764; Bentham, 1789) that asserted individuals commit criminal acts when the benefits outweigh the potential costs or consequences of offending. Crouch (1993) found that many inmates in fact prefer prison to the streets because it provides a comparatively comfortable setting. Many quantitative researchers identify the relationship between adaptation and inmate age concerning the experiences of incarceration. Shover's (1985) longitudinal study demonstrated that older inmates have more experience with incarceration than younger individuals and usually have been offended throughout their life course. Crank (2014) found that age and experience have specific links to inmates' ability to adapt. Younger prisoners are less likely to find confinement brutal, while older inmates are more likely to find prison time. Older inmates can adapt with less difficulty than younger inmates because older individuals are more likely to have learned the systems and means to adjust physically and mentally to prison, mostly avoiding potential trouble by identifying dangerous situations (Shover, 2018). Former inmates may have been exposed to similar rules and ways of life in other contexts, and therefore adapt to prison with ease (May et al., 2008). Shover (2018) stated that older prisoners begin to wonder if their remaining years of life are wasted at varying incarceration stages. Therefore, they value the remaining years more highly than they did previously. At certain junctures, they may begin to accept that significant changes in their views and lifestyle must be made. The results demonstrate the non-linear relationship between age and adaptation.

Crank (2015) found that age and experience have specific links to inmates' ability to adapt. Shover's (2018) results indicate that age and experience positively influence prison adjustment among older men serving sentences. Shover's (2018) report stressed that scholars should not rely on public or official perceptions of adaptation to prison life because those perceptions seem to lead to misguided correctional policies. It is more important to consider the offenders' opinions and research findings regarding the criminal justice system. The importance of offenders' perspective on adaptation and intention to avoid criminal behavior to date remains understudied on actual prisoners.

Life in prison is a punishing, painful existence (Sykes, 1958). Despite this, inmates can use their time constructively through mature adaptation and coping strategies (Johnson, 2002). Irwin (2009) noted that every form of adaptation has strategy elements, and the strategies are mutually exclusive. Irving also suggested that prisoners employ different adaptation techniques during various stages of their imprisonment. Further, they may select some aspects of multiple adaptation styles and apply them simultaneously.

Lambregts (2020) in a review of an address by Ben Crewe, described Dr. Crewe as a critical figure in penology. Dr. Ben Crewe delivered a lecture on October 27, 2020, at the All-Souls Criminology Seminar in Cambridge on long-term imprisonment and raised a broad range of humanistic issues. Crewe named challenges that are unique to sentence lengths of 15 years or longer and how prisoners adapt to those challenges and suggested that surveys and in-depth interviews are needed for prisoners to describe their experiences. He found that the results differed for male and female prisoners and, most importantly, prisoners during different incarceration stages. Early stages of imprisonment are characterized by higher severity issues than those in the mid-stage. Those at later stages exhibit lower commitments to early stages of incarceration and fewer mental health issues, along with less severe problems in general. Overall, prisoners develop ways of adapting to their circumstances and the challenges of isolation from the outside world. This later stage is what Johnson (2002) termed mature coping. Crewe et al. (2020) explained that the results of in-depth interviews provided more detail regarding prisoners' transitional phases during incarceration.

Archer (2003) discussed prisoners' transition from the initial states of shame, grief, and shame to inner conversations that reflect how inmates should act with their self-designed end goals in mind. Crewe et al. (2020) cited Archer (2003) as providing a valuable framework for understanding how long-term prisoners deal with the shock of their new circumstances and how they adopt a sense of self and explore life with possibilities. Archer (2003) discussed prisoners' transition from the initial states of shame, grief, and shame to inner conversations that reflect how they should act with their self-designed end goals in mind. Archer defined five transitional stages of adaptation: adapting to the sentence, perception of time, control and self-control, coming to terms with the offense, and finding purpose. Crewe et al. (2017) also described the early transitional stages as shifting from reactive agency to a productive phase. He used a metaphor of "swimming with the tide." Long-term prisoners move from initial backward-looking swimming *against* the tide to productive future-oriented use of swimming *with* the tide as an aid. He also noted that his study introduced a novel humanistic approach.

Smoyer et al. (2019) stated that most existing research on long-term sentences addressed prison stakeholders' rather than inmates' perspectives. Di Lorito et al. (2018) analyzed data collected directly from prisoners and formerly incarcerated older adults rather than stakeholders (p. 253). They identified 25 papers, of which 16 were qualitative; only two of these concerned older adults' lived experiences, and those articles were not peer-reviewed. As a result of this gap in existing knowledge, members of Miszewski (2017) reported that there are two famous typologies of adaptation to incarceration, identified by Goffman (1961) and Irwin (1997). Goffman (1961) noted that there are five strategies of adaptation:

- Playing it cool, which is an indication of acceptance without action, i.e., joining in without revealing any insecurities.
- Situational withdrawal, meaning a reaction will depend on the situation and can vary.
- Conversion, which is acceptance of the problem and the following suit.
- Intransigent line, meaning not to agree and not accept change
- Colonization, which means taking charge of the environment in the situation at hand and asserting your dominance.

Irwin (1997) believed that prison adaptation is flexible. He claimed that every form of adaptation has various strategies, and the strategies are mutually exclusive. Irwin contended that many prisoners utilize different adaptation techniques during the various stages of their imprisonment, or they may select some aspects of varying adaptation styles and apply them simultaneously.

On a more practical level, the advice from a welcome card given to new members of the Gray Panthers Organization at a maximum-security prison provides examples of some conventional adaptation techniques: "Say less. When in doubt, say nothing at all. Look, but do not stare ... Choose your words wisely ... Blend in with your clothes ... Stay off the gate when you are locked in your cell; agree with correction officers." For the proposed study, using adaptation theory as a theoretical framework will facilitate a narrative exploration of how older men with long-term sentences adapt and adjust to prison life, and the catalysts and outcomes of these decision-making points.

Conclusions from Literature Review

This portion of the book reviewed existing studies concerning adjustment and adaptation. The studies highlighted internal and external factors but generally overlooked the inmates' perspectives. Further, there is limited research on long-term inmates as well as the role of aging. The present study provides first-person perspectives on adaptation and adjustment among long-term inmates garnered from interviews.

Understanding positive adjustment and adaptation of long-term inmates through interviews will enable the identification of significant determinants for positive behaviors and behavioral supports. Adaptation and adjustment are vital factors in understanding the prosocial changes long-term inmates often undergo.

Purpose of the Study

The primary objective of my dissertation study was to understand perspectives and experiences regarding adaptation and adjustment among older men with life sentences in the United States. Further, my goal was to provide insight into the positive psychological and social effects of adaptive processes. I utilized face-to-face interviews to collect qualitative data describing lived experiences and first-person narratives from older men serving life sentences in order to understand how they adjust and adapt during their prison experience. The current lack of attention to the older men's LWOP incarceration experience in most studies has muted their collective voices. What is needed is an understanding of how to meet their needs better, and the use of such knowledge in the development of potential interventions (Haugebrook et al., 2010). This study's findings can inform both practice and theory around the imprisonment of older men in the United States, and help instigate changes to prison policy, programming, and research.

Scope and Limitations

This study was designed to collect, explore, and understand the narratives of older men serving life sentences in maximum-security prisons. The data included observations during interviews as inmates respond to semi structured interview questions. Simultaneously, I noted context, language, behavior, an interviewee's appearance, and their demeanor. The participants were all over 50 years of age and had served a minimum of twenty-five years of maximum-security incarceration.

As with any study that looks at only a small set of people, there is a need for caution in applying or generalizing the results to other specific groups or populations. For example, this study's findings do not necessarily apply to female LWOPs or prisoners serving other types of sentences. Nonetheless, this research was conducted in such a manner as to enhance the possibility of transferability. This research focused on the inmate population's perspectives rather than those of correction officials, legislators, politicians, guards, and/or other stakeholders. I remained mindful of the possible influence of my experience and views and attempted to take account of this in the interpretation of the results.

I sought to mitigate the possibility of participants' false statements by stressing the importance of honest and detailed explanations. Researchers seek to promote candid answers by openly discussing the value of honesty, and through documents presented to, and signed by, the participants.

I remained aware of the possible limitations due to research bias, and to credibility issues in the subjective data analysis. These issues are inherent in a qualitative study (Creswell, 2015). The interviews examined the adjustments and adaptations which occurred from the viewpoints of the incarcerated. As a former member of the Prison Society, I had to be constantly aware of potential bias. At all times, as the researcher, I had to be mindful of credibility issues because of the subjectivity involved in historical research. Further, I am involved in Prison Society by providing pro-bono instructions on the commutation process. Therefore, I set myself the goals of objectivity, remaining mindful of potential bias, staying true to the interview plan, and distancing myself to remain objective (Georgi, 2009). My study proposal was also reviewed by my peers and dissertation chair with an eye toward uncovering any avoidable bias.

CHAPTER 3

....

Research Method

This study explored the views of older men sentenced to life in prison and gained insight into inmates' perspectives on adjustment and adaptation while incarcerated. The results of this study portrayed the narratives of incarcerated older men, explaining their adjustment, adaptation, or maladaptation during their lengthy incarceration in a maximum-security prison. This study explored the perspectives of those serving life. As Tonry (2011) stated, these are primarily issues of human rights and social justice. These inmates made valuable contributions and have the potential to contribute to a healthier prison climate. In Chapter 3, I describe this qualitative study's research design and illustrate the methodology, data collection plan, research questions, and data analysis procedures. To achieve rigor, validity, and credibility, this study was structured so that the data matches the research questions' contexts and is aligned with the overall project. Other areas of concern were trustworthiness, bias, and ethical considerations (Patton, 2010).

Research Design and Rationale

The following research questions were used to guide this study:

- RQ1: What are the narratives of adaptation and adjustment in older men with life sentences?
- RQ2: How do older men with life sentences describe their present and ongoing adaptation and adjustment experience?

The rationale for this qualitative study's research design was that I believed that more pertinent information and data would be discovered by exploring the inmates' perspectives on long-term imprisonment, as stated by Di Lorito et al. (2018). This was accomplished by conducting face-to-face interviews involving semi structured and open-ended questions designed to elicit views and opinions from the participants. As stated by Crank (2010), existing literature has consisted mainly of other stakeholders' perspectives. According to Patton (2002), it was vital to ensure reflexivity in the data collection process. To accomplish this goal, I used interviews in alignment with the research questions. Using a qualitative research method, this study provided an understanding of the phenomena of adjustment and adaptation through the participants' life stories. Because those serving LWOP sentences have rarely been considered, it was essential to add their perspectives to compare or contrast the stakeholders' opinions that appeared in most research. The results provided rich, detailed descriptions and may hopefully be transferable to future research endeavors.

Role of the Researcher

My role as a researcher was to function as an observer, interviewer, and prominent instrument in this qualitative research study. First, I was physically present with the participants; in qualitative research, it is necessary to hold interviews in a comfortable, private, and convenient location and observe and record the perspectives and behaviors (Glense, 2016). Second, for the results to be stable and ensure that they produce meaning concerning inmates' experiences, the research was analytic and descriptive. As qualitative research is inductive, theories emerged from concepts and methods derived from the contextualized data (Cannella & Lincoln, 2012). There was no power over the participants as instruction was not graded and was a voluntary instructional self-improvement class for the inmates. My association was more formal as a member of the Prison Society. As the researcher, I did not influence inmates' participation or nonparticipation in the research process. Third, I made deliberate choices to account for potential bias. In this study, it was essential to recognize that collaboration, rigor, criticality, and reflexivity were vital to establishing ethical and valid reviews after reviewing the archival records of over 900 older male inmates serving LWOP. I was given access to the lifer's history as part of their commutation applications, containing data to formulate my interview questions. I eliminated those with educational, literacy, and language deficiencies to ensure credibility. Fourth, I ensured ethical considerations; I did not select participants until after receiving a list of potential participants from the Department of Corrections for reference.

Methodology

The men invited to participate in this study were all inmates of Graterford State Correctional Facility in Eastern Pennsylvania. The population includes over 900 older males serving LWOP.

Figure 1

Outside Security at SCI Phoenix, the Expansion Facility of Graterford Prison

Note. The old lock and key doors, which are still in use at Graterford, have been replaced by electronic, centrally monitored cell doors and gates, cameras, and sensors. The perimeter of SCI Phoenix is surrounded by a double ring of fences with razor wire, cameras, and sensors. Yes, a modern facility but plagued with mx issues and learning issues for the correctional officers unfamiliar with computer driven surveillance.

The Department of Corrections prepared a recommended list and referred it to the prison's primary "old-timers' organization" for review. The Graterford Gray Panthers is an organization granted a charter by Maggie Kuhn after she visited the prison in 1980. She tasked the members to continue in her goal of achieving representation for seniors in need. The list included 25 older male inmates who fit the interview criteria. The criteria were males over age 50 and confined for more than 25 years. The criteria also included sufficient educational, literacy, and language skills for meaningful engagement in the research. No incentives are permitted within the Pennsylvania Department of Corrections, so none were necessary for this research. I remained nonbiased and therefore assigned an alphanumeric designator to each name to assure confidentiality. As this was a purposeful random sample, I then placed each of the 25 balls marked with the designator into a metal bingo ball drawing tumbler. The first 10 numbers selected from the bingo cage became the participants selected for the study. I remained aware of the possible limitations stated by Creswell (2015) that research bias and credibility issues are inherent in a qualitative study because the data analysis was interpreted through subjective interpretations. The interviews and observations were used to examine the adjustments and adaptations which occurred from the viewpoints of the incarcerated. An alphanumeric identifier was assigned to each name, and 10 names were randomly selected for participation.

Inclusion and Exclusion Criteria

The selected 10 older male participants, all over age 50 and all confined for more than 25 years, provided their perspectives. This focused the inmates' perspectives more accurately and reflected the actual adjustments and adaptations as encountered. Women inmates were excluded due to the inability to gain permission to enter the women's facility and the relatively small numbers of women incarcerated in Pennsylvania compared to the male inmates. There was also the question of the transferability and dependability of data when combining male and female participants. The existing literature's transferability was limited due to the sparseness of research in the United States, as most studies have been conducted in Great Britain. Very few have been published on women serving life sentences.

Instrumentation

The study encompassed a review of inmate commutation proposals. The commutation proposal included pre-incarceration information and current information on the proposed participants' activities and eliminated the need for extensive questioning about the participants' mindset early on in their imprisonment. This required a series of initial interviews, letters, coding, theming, and data, as well as a second interview and in some cases a third interview to assure truthfulness, validity, ethics, and approval by the participants (see Appendices for interview guide). The maximum-security prison environment prohibited audio or video recording of inmates. However, due to the COVID-19 virus epidemic, Prison Society members, such as myself, were permitted to utilize video visitation.

Procedures for Recruitment, Participation, and Data Collection

Data collection commenced upon receipt of Walden Institutional Review Board (IRB) approval. As stated earlier, the interviews followed this format. A list of candidates was provided and vetted, and an additional effort, if needed, at a snowball sampling method, was utilized within the approved list of candidates. The data collection instruments were as follows: archival records of the inmates' application for commutation provided the pre-incarceration history and descriptions of previous crimes and current offenses leading to incarceration. The review of the commutation application or request for clemency was essential to provide me with a pre-imprisonment background, which aided in the preparation of interview questions. The Department of Correction granted me permission to review and research in January 2020, which allowed me to review the commutation applications with background on all participants. Utilizing this archival material eliminated hours of interview time by having pertinent data in advance of the interview process and aided in my design of the interview's semi-structured questions. Each participant was contacted via email and General Telephone (GTL) phone system and given an overview of what was expected of them and what they could expect from me as the sole researcher. This initial process filtered down the number of potential participants. According to the Department of Corrections (DOC) regulations and viewpoints, those names were then cleared with the DOC for suitability. Following the

DOC approvals and rejections, the remaining list was sent to the Graterford Gray Panthers Organization, responsible for managing and protecting the senior inmates.

I then commenced with initial written letter interviews with 10 separate participants, selected for data collection inclusion. I then emailed items that required clarification to the inmates to prepare for the second interview. A final interview, if needed, was scheduled two weeks after the second interview to review the initial two interview conclusions and enable the participant to edit and make any necessary additions or deletions. As a result, my first interview with the participants was via a letter containing the seven interview questions. Afterward, I used inmates' answers and notes to accurately portray the inmates' perspectives. During the initial meeting, I encouraged the participants to remain involved, to email, or send letters to me, the researcher, to add to or delete any of their thoughts before the closing interview. The participants were between the ages of 55 and 85, and currently incarcerated at a maximum-security prison. The data collected from this narrative study yielded information in the research notes, emails, and letters combined with the personal data and information available from the commutation application and the inmates' records. I endeavored to describe and identify specific patterns and themes from the participants' perspectives. Therefore, a comprehensive understanding and explanation of designs and themes emerged.

Trustworthiness

It was essential to understand that truthfulness and objectivity are key to the study. It was crucial to illustrate the believability and trustworthiness of the research through verification rather than traditional reliability and validity measures (Creswell, 2015). I considered participant anonymity, confidentiality, and informed consent. I focused on exercising ethical reflexivity and avoiding harm and bias. I focused on ethics regarding informed consent and participants' ability to withdraw from the voluntary study with no consequences. The essential aspect was to address all the ethical considerations. When discussing sensitive information, I respected the values and desires of the participants, whose lives we are researching and invading. This is particularly relevant when dealing with individuals in this population, because of the participant's status as a lifer and his actions are evident within the Department of Corrections. While objectivity and truthfulness were critical, I sought believability and trustworthiness, which I facilitated through verification processes, instead of the traditional textbook validity and reliability measures.

Credibility

The key to credibility is neutrality. According to Patton (2002), the researcher must not have a predetermined or vested interest or prejudice. A good strategy for credibility was to seek honest and empirically supported findings while adopting a neutral stance. Patton (2002) also explained the importance of triangulation, which increased credibility and quality, so the study findings are not just the result of a single method. He also discussed reflexivity, which I found relevant in dealing with minority and vulnerable participants who might find it suspicious that a member of another culture (i.e., the dominant culture) researched people of an oppressed group. Probst and Berenson (2014) explained that reflexivity was usually understood as an awareness of the researcher's influence and how the process affects the researcher. They claimed that reflexivity was both a state of mind and a set of actions. The researcher must not manipulate data to prove a particular perspective. The researcher must strive to understand the data as it unfolds and remain balanced in reporting positive and negative evidence regarding the conclusion.

Transferability

Transferability in qualitative research has to do with generalizability and external validation. According to Merriam (2016), transferability is concerned with the extent and way a research study can be applicable or applied to other studies or situations. Because of the qualitative nature of this study, generalizability cannot occur in a statistical sense. However, the methodology is certainly transferable. The researcher's job is to provide a thick description and enough detail in any context to enable a reader to compare and fit for their situations, as stated by Merriam (2016); it is the reader who must decide whether the findings can apply to their specific situation.

Dependability

According to Patton (2015), alternative sets of criteria are offered when discussing the issue of reliability in qualitative research. Depending upon the type of research, he suggested criteria for (a) traditional scientific, (b) constructivist, (c) artistic, (d) complexity, (e) participatory, (f) critical, and (g) pragmatic/utilization-focused research. To have effect, the research study must have rigor, present insights, and be something a reader can believe. As this research goal was to understand, I discovered that my trust criteria differed from those needed for testing a hypothesis.

Confirmability

Whether or not the research I was observing was measuring what it has been designed to measure, became an issue. What was being studied, and how did I assess the validity of my observations? Given that these were the primary instruments of my data collection and analysis, it was necessary to access them directly. The research must contain thick and rich descriptions. Patton (2015) described a thick story as being detailed and highly descriptive. It is presented as describing the setting, and the findings and supporting evidence of the interview process presented as a participant's narrative quotation. If the study were viewed in this research type, it became vigorous, providing the strength for qualitative analysis. Confirmability was needed to understand the complexity of inmates' behavior. Therefore, I presented the study as a holistic interpretation of what was occurring.

Treatment of Data

I, as researcher, and the type of research I performed, respected the dignity and, more importantly, the privacy of vulnerable participants. Therefore, information collected during the research process was protected. I utilized reasonable precautions to maintain confidentiality. All data was stored on a computer hard drive and backup thumb drives and was encrypted with designated security. The encrypted dated was password-protected, and firewall-secured. None of the data was subject to emails, fax, or was electronically transmitted. All data was kept in the researcher's private office, secured by alarms and motion detectors, and has fire-proof locking files.

The steps to protect the data collected consisted of utilizing participant codes on all collected material and data analysis. Any records linking the participant codes to any personal identifiers were kept in a secure file that I could destroy when no longer needed. Also, separate consent forms of collected material avoided participant identification. I remained aware of the disclosures permitted by law, as well as of my obligation regarding the duty-to-protect laws in this jurisdiction.

This qualitative research relied on unstructured data. A study may utilize different methods such as interviews and questionnaires, field notes, observation, audio, or video recordings carried out in natural settings, and archival documents used in psychology. This research builds on existing literature and extends the existing knowledge which utilized handwritten interviews and realized threats to validity when dealing with vulnerable populations. I focused on confidentiality in this research, as carried out within this vulnerable group.

Summary

Chapter 3 consisted of the methods used to explain the research design and rationale, the methodology, recruitment, participation, and data collection procedures used. The chapter also included essential elements, such as various trustworthiness issues, namely, credibility, transferability, dependability, and confirmability, along with a detailed data analysis plan.

The chapter concluded with the summary and a thorough examination of ethical procedures: institutional permission, including IRB approvals and Pennsylvania Department of Corrections institutional approval. The last element with ethical concerns dealt with the vulnerable population and the program's participation or withdrawal.

CHAPTER 4

....

Results

This research utilized qualitative methods of research designs. Patton (2007) claimed that to understand what something means to a participant, the researcher should pursue a qualitative research study to gather their experiences and stories. This qualitative analysis explored the adaptation and adjustment of older men serving life in a maximum-security prison. The data described the men's lived experiences from their perspectives. Because most of the past research relied on stakeholders' data and neglected the necessary subjectivity, which can only be achieved by revealing the views of the men incarcerated, it is essential and relevant to note that extant literature described experiences of loss, abuse, the dangers of prison, and a lack of medical concern. Therefore, the existing research is deficient in that positive aspects of inmates' adaptation and adjustment have been overlooked or ignored.

This research centered on the voices of older male prisoners serving life sentences and tells their stories. It will also inform stakeholders of possible interventions in support of this vulnerable population. Chapter 4 includes the demographics, research setting, data analysis, data collection, evidence of trustworthiness, results, and a detailed summary.

Setting

I know of no personal or disclosed organizational conditions that influenced participants or their experience at the time of study that may affect the interpretation of the study results. This research setting within a maximum-security prison in Pennsylvania required written permission from the Department of Corrections Bureau of Planning, Research, and Statistics. The location was altered from the earlier proposal of the face-to-face interview due to the COVID-19 restriction, which prevented face-to-face meetings. The institution ended all visitations and predicted that the shut-down might exceed one year. However, the institution permitted me to proceed with the study using email and U.S. mail correspondence. The COVID-19 was deemed a pandemic and anticipated to last over a year, which forced me to obtain approval from the Department of Corrections to modify my methodology, and all data were collected through the U.S. mail and emails.

Demographics

The participants are all men between the ages of 55 and 85 and are currently incarcerated at a maximum-security prison. They were imprisoned for virtual life sentences or LWOP and had been confined for a minimum period of 25 consecutive years. However, all but one participant had been incarcerated for over 35 years. The participants' offenses included drug offenses, burglary, robbery, assault, gun violations, and murder. A few of the demographics of the participants are shown in Table 1.

Table 1

Demographics of the Participants

Participant	Age	Education	Years in prison
1 TR 111	57	PhD	27
2 SM 112	70	BA	40
3 ER 113	67	GED	41
4 SB 114	85	BA	47
5 BB 115	65	BA	41
6 CR 116	70	GED	40
7 LS 117	72	AB	48
8 BR 118	68	BA	46
9 KL 119	65	GED	42
10 DG 110	76	HS	38

Procedure

Graterford is a maximum-security facility and does not permit the audio or video recordings of inmates. Due to the COVID-19 epidemic, no in-person contact was allowed. However, as a member of the Prison Society, I was granted video visitation.

I also had access to the inmates' written applications for commutation. The applications provided the pre-incarceration history and descriptions of previous crimes and current offenses leading to incarceration. The review of the commutation application or request for clemency was essential to provide me with a pre-imprisonment background and aided in the preparation of interview questions. Utilizing this archival material eliminated hours of interview time by having pertinent data in advance of the interview and aided in my design of the interview's semi-structured questions.

The first study contact was a questionnaire in letter format. It contained seven primary interview questions. The participants could take as much time as they wished to respond. I then emailed individuals about items that required clarification, and to prepare them for the second interview. A final interview, if needed, was scheduled two weeks after the second interview. It was done to review the earlier interviews' content and allow the participants to edit their answers and make any necessary additions or deletions. During the initial meeting, I encouraged the participants to remain involved and to email or send letters to me, the researcher, to edit any of their responses before the closing interview. In the closing interviews, the participants reviewed the research data and conclusions. I felt that the extensive communications with the participants increased the trustworthiness and reliability of the data collected. The format encouraged the participants to go beyond their initial reactions to the research questions. Through the use of the open-ended semi-structured question format, and by revisiting their responses, the data became richer and more nuanced.

Participant Confidentiality

In the United States, it is required that any proposed research that involves human participants (subjects) be reviewed by a Human Subjects Review Board. Colleges and universities with research programs of any kind that involve humans as research subjects are therefore required to submit research protocols to the Institutional Review Board's (IRB) review.

The purpose of IRB review is to assure, both in advance and by periodic review, that appropriate steps are taken to protect the rights and welfare of humans participating as subjects in the research. To accomplish this purpose, IRBs use a group process to review research protocols and related materials (e.g., informed consent documents and investigator brochures) to ensure protection of the rights and welfare of human subjects of research. (https://www.fda.gov/about-fda/center-drug-evaluation-and-research-cder/institutional-review-boards-irbs-and-protection-human-subjects-clinical-trials)

The inmates who volunteered for this study were from a stigmatized group and feared being "found out" for being critical of guards or the prison operations in general. As a result, I did not disclose what the inmates said or did during the research study without their consent. The most critical factor in dealing with these participants was to assure and maintain confidentiality. To achieve this, my interviews and notes remained confidential. The main issue was never to identify any of the participants. The primary step to protect anonymity consisted of utilizing participant codes on all collected material and during data analysis. Any records linking the participant codes to personal identifiers are in a secure file that I can destroy when no longer needed.

As part of my efforts to reassure the participants of the confidentiality and safety of their responses, I utilized a back-and-forth approach. During data collections, opportunities for review, clarification and editing were provided to the participants. The analysis of the research was also presented to each participant for review. They had the right to make additions, corrections, and deletions. I also considered the research transcripts and how changes, such as they made, affected the response authenticity, and resulted in data loss. This issue was discussed with participants before they volunteered for the project. Most said they would not edit the content and wanted the research to be truthful and reliable.

Interview Questions

Research that uses open-ended questionnaires and interviews is called *qualitative research*. In qualitative research, non-numerical data (e.g., text, video, or audio) is used to understand concepts, opinions, or experience. It is not looking for cause and effect. Instead, the goal is to survey an area of concern and discover the most prevalent themes and issues. By contrast, in *quantitative research* the topic of interest is explored by obtaining measurements (i.e., quantifiable data) and then applying statistical, mathematical, or computational techniques to compare or describe variables of interest. The present study used a qualitative approach.

After studying the existing literature about the role of adaptation in prison, I wanted to focus on the positive psychological and social effects of the adaptive processes among older men with life sentences in the United States. My goal was to understand perspectives and experiences of the prisoners with regard to adaptation and adjustment. I formulated the two primary research questions (RQs) more precisely as follows:

- RQ1: What are the narratives of adaptation and adjustment in older men with life sentences?
- RQ2: How do older men with life sentences describe their present and ongoing adaptation and adjustment experience?

With these goals in mind, I created a set of seven interview questions. Each question consisted of multiple sentences and was designed to elicit thoughts and opinions around a particular topic. The questions are shown in Table 2.

Table 2

Interview Questions

Number	Question
	Tell me how you felt once you were initially incarcerated. What was it like for you? What was the main thing that helped you adapt to being in prison?
2.	You have been in prison for decades; please describe your primary source of motivation. How would you describe how you have changed?
3.	How did this source change the way you looked at the fact you were in prison for life? How would you describe how you have adapted to being in prison? What has helped you adjust to being in prison on this type of sentence?
4.	How do you feel about life generally? What is in the future for you? How do you look at the years ahead? Do you have a prediction?
5.	When a person makes up his mind to go straight, it is usually due to what we call a hook. Please tell me what your hook was and describe how this turning point changed your ways.
6.	Tell me about your best and worst experience serving a life sentence.
7.	Looking back over the many years you have been in prison, what do you think helped you most to adapt to prison life, and what keeps you going today?

In the last step of the procedure the final draft of this report and the analysis of the research were presented to each participant for review. More often than not, they made stylistic comments and corrections to their statements and requested certain deletions of what I consider exciting text segments. They had the right to make such additions, corrections, and deletions. However, I also considered the research transcripts and how such changes affected the text's authenticity and whether they resulted in data loss. However, this issue was discussed with participants before their volunteering for the project. Most stated they would not edit the content and would like the research to be truthful and reliable.

How the Data Was Analyzed

I used a narrative analysis to record, observe, and analyze the stories that emerged. The goal was to understand the meaning of the experiences reported. The data collected from this study included research notes, emails, and letters combined with personal data and information available from the commutation application and the inmates' records. The goal was to describe and identify specific patterns and themes from the participants' perspective. Therefore, a comprehensive understanding and explanation of patterns and themes emerged. The data were organized and coded. The videotaped interviews, if any, were transcribed verbatim and combined with the field notes and diary entries. The data were entered into a computer program called HyperQual for contrast and comparison. With this analysis software, the necessary categories and code names were organized into categories, words, phrases, and themes.

For this research project I relied solely on intra-coding. Inter-coding was not utilized because of this vulnerable population's confidentiality, privacy, and ethical considerations. I performed line-by-line hand-coding while paying particular attention to covert meanings that resided within my transcribed interview.

However, I also utilized a secondary coding source for a comparative purpose, which was computer coding from one of the prominent providers of the software. The software programs were *ATLAS-ti; Ethnography; HyperRESEARCH; NVivo; SuperHyperQual; Transana;* and these other entries: *Axial Coding; Codes and Coding; Computer-Assisted Data Analysis; Content Analysis; Document Analysis; Ethnographic Content Analysis; In Vivo Coding; Open Coding; Selective Coding; Thematic Coding and Analysis.* Computer coding assisted the research effort in that it achieved a higher stage and refinement of coding.

Data Collection

The study began after receiving Walden University IRB approval (Approval no. 04-30-21-0584753) in June 2021. The data collection was completed in July 2021. The Pennsylvania Department of Corrections provided a list (filtered to meet my criteria) of male inmates who met the study's initial requirements. Female inmates were excluded from the project due to the Pennsylvania Department of Corrections policy. I then sent a flyer to each of the potential participants explaining the research. After receiving positive acceptance signatures, I requested their willingness to participate in the study, sent to me via U.S. Mail. I began to receive correspondence from my flyer almost immediately (within one week), and after receiving the first 25, I determined that I had received enough responses, so I decided to proceed. To ensure that I remained nonbiased, I assigned an alphanumeric designator to each name to assure confidentiality. I then placed each of the 25 balls marked with the designator into a metal bingo ball drawing tumbler wire cage. The first 10 numbers selected from the bingo cage became the participants selected for the study.

I then sent the willing participants the documentation required by Walden IRB, which included the necessary letter of intent stressing privacy and confidentiality. My primary collection method was through U.S. mail with each of the 10 participants, to each of whom I wrote a letter. The letter contained seven semi-structured open-ended questions. A second letter with follow-up was sent as required when further information was needed. Due to confidentiality issues, I performed data collection myself.

Once responses to the interview questions were received, with the limitations placed on all visitations due to the COVID-19 pandemic, I calculated that time to secure the letter-writing would require only 5 weeks, and therefore the letter-writing process became an effective alternative. This change from interview to letter-writing methodology was discussed and agreed to by my committee members. All respondents' (the first 25 to respond) names were placed in a hat, and I selected 10 participants. My committee chairperson agreed that 10 participants would be adequate for saturation and obtaining data. The smaller sample size was conducive to getting a richer exploration than I would have otherwise achieved by a larger sample within the time allotted for analysis.

There were no time constraints with letter writing, and the participants could take as much or as little time as desired or required. Unlike face-to-face interview, the participants had time to reflect on the questions and to consider their responses without any pressure to offer an immediate response. As a result, this change, organizational conditions, and existing incarceration trauma had no adverse influence on the study results or interpretation.

Qualitative methods allowed me to explore various issues in depth, with data collection permitting me to view my participants' points of view without bias, preconceived concepts, or predetermining their perspectives. This methodology provided a wealth of detailed information. Moreover, it led me to a deep understanding of the long-term prisoners' life experiences. As Creswell (2013) stated, qualitative studies have an arcane number of choices of methods; thus, I felt qualitative was the best method to achieve my goals.

Data Analysis

I used a narrative method for this study. Participant response letters usually included three to ten text pages and totaled over 120 pages for all ten inmates. The coding became an arduous yet vital task. Initially, I had difficulty making sense of the data. Table 3 illustrates categories/themes that each of the respondents enumerated by alphanumeric designation to the interview questions listed in the seven columns.

Under each interview question is the number designating the theme extracted. Each participant was asked identical questions in the same order. The response to each research question led to the coding by described phrases and words into the eight subthemes derived from the codes found.

As I arrived at a category or theme, I sent the second letter out to the inmates to further explain responses that were unclear, vague, or required more explanation. To do this, I immersed myself in the data and consolidated the data on Excel spreadsheets. Hand coding was tedious, and I had to compare segments looking for categories/themes in the data. This was more difficult because I needed to understand what was written and the meaning of the pattern/themes. These meanings or understandings became my study's findings. Various themes emerged; 10 participants were sufficient because the size was conducive to rich, in-depth exploration than would have been possible with larger groups.

Table 3

Categories and Themes from Interview Data

	ID	Subtheme Name
Theme 1: Adaptation to prison by LWOPs	1 A	Fear
	1 B	Isolation
	1 C	Survival
Theme 2: Strategies of adaptation	2 A	Religiosity
	2 B	Aging/Maturity
	2 C	Education
	2 D	Family
	2 E	Hope

Evidence of Trustworthiness

This report unmasks how prisoners in a maximum-security prison adapt and adjust to their sentences. It reveals the perceptions of actual inmates with data collected from 10 older men serving life or life-without parole. They disclosed from their own perspectives how they adapted and adjusted to trauma and deprivations while serving life and life without parole sentences.

Much of the relevant literature conducted by psychologists or sociologists is decades old. I look to the work of Clemmer from over 80 years ago:

> An adult is primarily the result of what he has learned through childhood and youth. Then, as adults, they are the aggregate of their experiences. Consequently, we may assume that any environment and every social experience will contribute to changes in people appropriate, then, to examine prisoners' attitudes before their incarceration as a tool for understanding their coping skills in prison (Clemmer, 1940, p. 1).

This study shed light on the truth of prison, how the lifers perceive their lives, how they have evolved into a person with values and interests, and why their growth ought to trigger a positive response from society in general.

Category/Theme 1: Adaptation to Prison for LWOPs

The one theme that emerged for RQ1 was adaptation to prison for LWOPs. The three subthemes were Fear, Isolation and Survival. The inmates must adjust and adapt to the new, violent environment of prison to survive. They live in constant fear. The adjustment takes time - some achieve this in a matter of weeks, some in months, many in years. They have two choices: (a) continue a criminal path and associate with others who remain criminally inclined, or (b) change their way and seek rehabilitation, redemption, and growth as a member of society. The adaptation of the inmate is the common goal of survival. They must adapt to life as demonstrated in subthemes 1A, 1B and 1C.

The one narrative response common among all 10 participants was surviving in prison while living in a state of fear of being assaulted and killed. Isolating themselves from others was the primary approach to overcoming fear and surviving. Hence the subthemes of Fear, Isolation and Survival. There did not appear to be a sequence to learning to cope with these challenges. Instead, they form a multi-faceted approach to the main theme of Adaptation.

Fear

Fear was inevitable, even for the hardcore criminal. The environment of the max-security prison breeds fear for everyone. It remains with the men no matter how long they are incarcerated. As they age in prison, they learn to cope by knowing the behavior necessary to negate potential problems and thus alleviate the fears. LS 117 expressed it clearly:

> I think it is impossible to be anything but scared to death in a max facility. I sure as hell was scared and still am today. Even though I have friends now, which we watch out for each other, I can sleep at night, but we still must worry about the yard and chow time. … For the last 47 years I have prayed to God to get me out of here alive[;] that is my only motivation[,] nothing else matters.

Of course, the main issue of fear is not only being mugged, but survival. SM 112, who described his crime as heinous, detailed his feelings of fear upon being incarcerated, stating that, "Once in prison, I felt fear and was afraid because I did not know what to expect from other prisoners because I committed a needless and heinous crime. It was violent without provocation." He later elaborated:

> The turning point or process of changing my ways began early in my incarceration. As soon as my cell door closed, I knew I did not ever want to repeat my crime ever. As the doors closed shut, I made a change. I was locked in, scared to death, and my conscience was my guide. No one seems to care or even ask, but I made up my mind to make corrections in my life. Regardless of my life sentence, I refused to languish in a moment of a wrong decision.

This illustrates that even the tough street guys begin to realize death is very possible. Adaptation to fear through isolation is seen as the path to survival.

Isolation

In the early years of incarceration, the men isolated for protection. They felt it was necessary for survival. Later, when they adjusted in a matter of weeks in most cases, they only isolated to read and study, because they had acclimated themselves to the prison environment. SB 14 stated:

> …never realizing there were guys tougher than me. I remained as much of a hermit as possible, as I learned to survive and overcome all the prison required of me. I had an inkling of what I needed to do to stay alive and how to act to gain as much benefit as possible in prison. Though Graterford prison is another dog-eat-dog environment, I learned enough to get by and survive.

Thankfully, I got single-celled and made my way successfully through the years. … Anxiety was only a factor for me for the first couple of years.

In some cases, anxiety overcomes the inmate, and he remains in his cell as much as possible. The study results found this theme as an unstated undercurrent running through most narratives.

Survival

The fear of getting killed while an inmate was constant and always on the minds of the inmates from day one to time of death. BR 118 described himself as,

>…a tough guy, a former army ranger and I thought I was prepared to protect myself, but it was different, it was weird, I was afraid and didn't want guys to mess with me, so I stayed alone and just stayed in my cell[,] did my thing and hoped for the best.

DG 110 also described an intense desire to survive:

>I learned to appreciate the loss of freedom and loss of family and friends and not to take what blessing I have for granted. I am taking every program I can get so they notice I want to change and want to come out of here and not die in a prison.

SB 114 said "I hope to go home one day[;] that is what I pray for along with my daughter. The worst thing is that I never see my family again and die in this forsaken hole." BB 115 shared, "I have no choice but to stay alive for my daughter who knows I am innocent. I stay alive for her and take it one day at a time." LS 117 summed it up when he stated:

>It is impossible to be anything but scared to death and to worry who is going to get to you[.] [I]n a max facility everyone is dangerous and a threat, so I was always ready to protect myself. I was scared from day one and I still live in fear.

Category/Theme 2: Strategies of Adaptation and Adjustment to Prison for LWOPs

The second research question (RQ2) was, "How do older men with life sentences describe their present and ongoing experience of adaptation and adjustment?" The subthemes found within this theme were Religiosity, Aging/Maturity, Education, Family, and Hope.

The strategies of adaptation and adjustment to prison for LWOPs are evident from reading the account of these inmates who exist in a sparse and violent environment and provide insight into their acquisition of resiliency. Maturing and aging have made them patient and aware of themselves as they gain self-growth. Both adaptation and hope are shown in all the participants' writings. They have adapted and seen the need for purpose in life. For some, their purpose is to provide service to the prison and to younger inmates. These participants avoid trouble and are always searching for a means to self-improve. Their hope for eventual freedom greatly shapes their adaptation.

In contrast, SB 114 questioned his need or ability for adaptation:

One day at a time … you don't adapt, you just deal with it because you can't let it take over your mind. Some things you can move on from … others you live with [for] the rest of your life. Prison made me grow up. I have been here since I was 22[,] and now I am 64. I learned to live in peace within this madness.

Similarly, SM 112 stated:

You can't let life in prison dictate your thinking and behavior. So, I use my time in prison as therapy, made all the major changes to correct my thinking. Because, I knew, somehow, I had the solution within me. I accepted the adjustments for my life. Yes, I did kill, and I ask for forgiveness every day with integrity[,] determined to give everyone respect.

Religiosity

The participants expressed a variety of denominational beliefs. The acceptance of a higher authority was prevalent in many of the responses. Interestingly, none described their newfound religion as the "hook" (central motivation) for transformation. One participant, LS 110, explained:

The years have been difficult, and all I can do is ask God to help me work through this terrible sentence. I am an innocent man, so I remain angry and confused. I ask God every day to help me through this terrible ordeal.

BB 115 stated "I was God-fearing and believed God would help me. I was angry and frustrated and began to stutter, but a priest hypnotized me and cured me. I hope God will let me get out of here alive." Another participant, BR 118, has become a dedicated Catholic and daily churchgoer and volunteers with the various pastors. He said:

My primary source of motivation has been the church. I believe miracles can happen. I have hope. No one wants to stay in prison. [Y]ou know [that] even though I go to church[,] I still needed to get drunk to survive[.] [T]he only goal is to get out of here. Other guys[,] who had no family [and were] raised on the streets or [in] foster[,] care take prison easy, but I had a normal life[,] so even being a tough guy [in] prison takes a toll. [M]y religion and getting old made me feel a little safer, but God doesn't save everybody.

According to ER 113:

Only God knows what the future holds. As a result, I look towards a future with optimism that things will change for the better. Just thank God who has kept me alive this long and keep praying he doesn't forget me.

TR 111 said:

When you hit rock bottom you get sick and tired of being stuck in your own mess. I was tired of not being in control of even my own thoughts and emotions. I learned to meditate on God's word and how to deal with my anger[,] learning about love, peace[,] and how to treat others.

SM 112 said that prison was terrifying to him, explaining:

> No matter how long you are here it gets worse rather than better. My reality didn't come into focus for three or four years and I regained my senses[,] but all I can think about is how to survive in prison and what is going to happen to be ahead. Fear of the unknown and visions of what happens to murderers has prolonged my anxiety as I languish in prison for decade after decade. I just can't accept this existence when I think of prison being my final residence on earth. [O]nly God can save me[;] I can think of no other solution.

KL 119 explained:

> I thought I could start to help others but that didn't fix the mistakes I made on the outside and all [I] can think is how time has passed me by. I have been very sick and as I lay think[ing] about dying in prison, I realize[d] prison don't make you a person[,] only God does. I try to believe we all ha[ve] good and bad in us. Some guys never try to change, and I try to show them the way. I have been in here over forty years, and I still have something worthwhile to give. God will show me the way and maybe even help me a little before I die.

Aging/Maturity

In some cases, aging does not bring maturity as evidenced by inmates with bad behavior. This was not the case with these participants. One criterion for inclusion in this study was no instances of bad behavior in decades of imprisonment. The theme of aging includes missing family, death of family members or friends, and maturation. Aging is thought of as a hook by many researchers, as is the death of a family member. However, this research did not find either aging nor death of a family member as a hook concept. Hence, these themes seem to be serving more as reinforcements than catalysts or hooks.

Aging and maturity were certainly relevant to six of the 10 participants. The reality is that aging over time yields maturity in most cases. Aging is also responsible for reflective thinking and self-evaluation. SM 112 summed-up aging and maturity concisely. His comments are a sign of maturity:

> As growth and maturity settled into my life, correlated actions and attitudes representing new thinking followed. The thought that I could remain imprisoned for life gave me the incentive to refute the label LWOP. The thrill of living precedes any discomfort a life in confinement imposes. I anticipated improving my life through hope, a willingness to transform this earthly bondage, and hope was significant to improving conditions in my environment. However, I make every effort to do the right thing now, whatever the circumstances.

BR 118 wrote:

> I made up my mind to go straight in 1984[,] thirty-eight years ago. I got some classes and programs done and realized what a waste I was making of my life. I was out of control with addictions and behavior. My dad die[d] that day in [']84 and that was my starting point. I want to do what it takes to get out of here and make something of myself. I want my kids to respect me for my change and I vow to never, never get involved in any crime of any kind.

LS 117 reinforced these sentiments. He spends his days researching prisonization and statistics:

> Brother John[,] [h]ere is my answer to the "Opinion" conversation. Several studies with supporting facts and statistics show that usually after the age of 40, individuals are on the downside of criminal behavior. Much of this is due to the maturing of these individuals and the assumptions of adult responsibilities, stable relationships, [e]ducation, employment, or just being worn out by the criminal culture. I hope this adds some substance to the conversation. Peace Be with You and all that's important to you.

Education

Programs in prison are helping to provide the power of knowledge to inmates. With this power, overcoming the past and enjoying a better quality of life are very achievable goals. Education in prison helps to give inmates a second chance. Inmates who participated in educational programs were less likely to commit a crime and return to incarceration within three years than those who did not participate in education. LS 117 credits education as paramount in his adaptation. He said:

> For the past 47 years, my prime motivation was to survive. I want to be a positive example for my children. I have changed my unruly behavior and I got my associate[']s and my bachelor's degree in sociology[,] and my change will always be a continuing work in progress.

BR 118 said:

> [I] found [that] constant work on my education from GED to BA kept me busy and surrounded me with others who were positive thinkers. That[,] along with my [C]atholic religion kept me so busy and my mind occupied[,] [that] I had no time nor the mind for trouble.

The lifers I interviewed found meaning in their lives and adapted to incarceration. Yes, prisonization does shape their routine as you adapt to the environment in which you exist (Dhami, 2017). I found that the lifers seemed to create their routines and shape the prison world to meet their basic needs. Moreover, many of the participants credited belief in a higher authority as a primary factor. For example, TR 111, an inmate sentenced to LWOP for murder, who reached an education level of PhD in Theology while incarcerated, described the progression of his adaptation. He started with a really difficult time, as did others. It was his first and only arrest. It involved the murder of his wife during a domestic dispute. While he claimed self-defense, he was not successful. After about three years of incarceration, he "went to the Bible" and religion for emotional relief. He also became a man who instigated the love of God in others while incarcerated and enabled his students to become better men. TR111 said: "My path to adaptation was difficult. and I changed through a learned belief due to the Bible for answers. I became baptized Christian and have dedicated me to growing spiritually, mentally, and emotionally."

SM 112 explained:

> In this situation, the hook for me was the pain and sadness I caused my family. I need to restore the trust I have destroyed by committing murder. I want to rebuild the relationship, let my actions and character show, and do my speaking by witnessing how I am today. As growth and maturity

[have] settled into my life[,] correlated actions and attitudes representing new thinking followed for sure. The thoughts that I will remain imprisoned for life give me the incentive to refute the label LWOP[.] [I] have lost my family and most of my friends[,] so the only thing giving me hope is my newfound maturity[.] I guess it is part of growing old.

Family

This subtheme involved missing family and the death of family members. The absence of family relationships was a major issue with most participants. The absence could be brought about either through death or by the inability to visit with family or friends. The Family subtheme is expressed differently by each participant. Some are facing loneliness and some need counselling. Others come to realize the hurt they caused their family. Although I do not see Family as the single hook, the theme was mentioned in 75% of participant responses. For example, BB 115 stated:

Thinking about my dad changed my life. I wanted to prove myself to him and my family. I was no longer an addict or alcoholic. I got my Education GED and a BA from Villanova and took any and every program or course I can. Sometimes you just don't get it until you lose it. My dad died and brought my wasted life into focus. I regained my senses and was tired of being a criminal and stuck in my own mess. I got control of my thoughts and learned the right way to treat others and they treated me back. Even though I may end up in prison as my final residence nothing inside me gives me acceptance of this existence[.] [M]y maturity has changed me as I am now a mature and pro-active thinker. First time in jail[,] and I just am getting older. I have no choice but to stay alive for my daughter who knows I am innocent. I stay alive for her and take it one day at a time.

Similarly, LS 117 explained:

For the past forty-seven years all I wanted was to stay alive and get out of here to show my grandchildren that I can change into a better man. I got my associate and bachelor's degrees in sociology and my changing will always be a work in progress, but I owe my family to see me as the man I am today.

DG 110 recounted:

I am an innocent man and got sentenced to life and it took everything out of me except my family['s] love. The cop set me up[;] my kids know it[,] so how can I adapt or adjust to that? I took a lot of classes and learned. So, knowing I am innocent and that my family knows[,] I just keep my faith and hope God can save me somehow.

Hope

Hope was the single most prevalent theme and was expressed by every inmate interviewed. It was something frequently on their minds. The hope of one day getting a chance to get free and prove they can be a better man is articulated in almost every interview. TR 111 seemed uncertain but optimistic and stated:

...cannot predict, I got my PhD in Theology and have become a preacher, teacher, and mentor, sharing what I have learned with the young men who have found themselves in prison. Today I have forgiven myself and love myself. I have learned a great deal throughout my incarceration.

SM 112 stated:

Every feeling I have uncovered over the decades of the plight of my incarceration has in some way influenced the character and conduct of the man before you, and it does me good to weigh in on the challenges I have endured. Although the question [that] faces me cause[d] me to reflect deeply on a past that is not desirable, moving forward is more exciting because of the noticeable self-gratifying growth I accomplished through patience and maturity.

ER 113 wrote, "I have a willingness to accept accountability for the taking of another man's life[;] God knows what the future holds." Likewise, LS 117 said:

It would be with me forever. This memory of my crime changed my life, and I want to do good if they give me a second chance. I have been here for 37 years and never got any violations or troubles. I will do the same if I get a chance outside. Nevertheless, even on the outside, I will never forget my crime.

SB 114 said, "I hope to go home one day[;] that is what I pray for along with my daughter. The worst thing is that I never see my family again and die in this forsaken hole." Another participant, BB 115, explained:

As time moved on, I adapted, I got a big picture view. I became a goal-oriented person setting landmarks to get from one point to another. I keep a glimmer of hope alive by relying [on] God and moral support from my family and other friends, but it is only a glimmer[.] I don't want my family to see me die in prison. I think about dying in here and have nightmares frequently.

CR 116 stated:

I will never commit another crime[.] I don't want to send negative messages to my daughter and family. [M]y children need to know [that] to err is human and I should be forgiven[,] at least that is my hope when I get out of here. Look[,] I have been here over forty years, who needs a hook? I only made one mistake in my life and here I am, and I am not a career criminal.

DG 110:

I will be liberated one day and start a process of building a healthy relationship with my family and the community[,] and within the next five years I will have my own cleaning business and continue to fight unjust incarcerations. Education and spiritual enlightenment inspired me to become a better man. I was only a child when I came to prison and had selfish ways about me. I learned to appreciate the loss of freedom and loss of family and friends and not to take what blessing I have for granted. I am taking every program I can get so they notice I want to change and want to come out of here and not die in a prison. Being away from my family eats me alive and I can't be home when someone dies.

Summary

The main goal of this research study was to discover through interviews how long-term inmates adapted and what motivated these prisoners to change their ways. The method was to analyze their open-ended responses and efforts to adjust and adapt, to make themselves desirable for commutation and parole after decades of incarceration. These results become evident by examining the inmates' behavior and achievements. They avoid troublesome behavior and take advantage of every opportunity for self-improvement.

The data were collected from 10 men serving LWOP. The results of being sentenced to LWOP, also known as DBI, are very similar to a virtual life sentence. However, with a virtual life sentence, the inmate is parole-eligible after a certain period of time depending on the term of his sentence served. LWOP is by far the most inhumane and the harshest prison sentence possible in the United States. The inmates serving this sentence are not eligible for parole. Parole by commutation is nonexistent. The result for LWOP inmates is that they will die in prison.

I found common themes in the men's responses. These themes highlighted their abilities to achieve positive adaptation and adjustment, find new meaning in life, and most importantly, sustain the hope for release and the ability to achieve a second chance. The questions I utilized sought a remedy from the men themselves, and therefore were open-ended and semi-structured. However, the participants' responses were not necessarily in sequential order or format and therefore confusing. The main goal of this research study was to discover through interviews if long-term inmates adapted and what motivated these prisoners to change their ways. The underlying rationale is that I believe more pertinent information and data would be discovered by exploring the inmates' perspectives on long-term imprisonment, rather than solely depending on shareholders' viewpoints.

The results of the interviews dispel the time-honored myth that lifers' behaviors deteriorate in prison, as stated by Di Lorito et al. (2018). Toch (1992) found that aging, and therefore maturing, in prison leads to inmates' gaining better self-control. Lifers make their sentences their own by choosing personal routines and going along with the institutional program, which they come to realize they cannot change. I found that they maintained control over their incarceration by spending much of their time in solitary pursuits. They also become more thoughtful and join life groups.

The interviews revealed that the inmates are not living their lives in a state of passivity. The pressures of prison life have not totally worn them down. All the participants proved to be resilient, had good psychological profiles, and had common pro-social attitudes. Time and aging stood out as vital to the adaptation process. While the adjustment process began slowly, it fed on itself with the passage of time. As the men learned more skills, they gained more confidence in themselves and acquired additional skills. All of the selected participants pursued educational programs while incarcerated, typically early in their sentences. While learning to read and write, they gained verbal intelligence and emotional security. According to Flanagan (1981), as they aged and participated in programs to improve, these men also demonstrated substantial reductions in violations and had no occurrences of hostility. They remain resilient in their pursuit and hold onto hope, stating that hope is crucial, which is no easy undertaking. Maruna (2004) called this "making good." By avoiding for decades in the case of my participants, they demonstrate persistence, deep faith and become aware that their behavior would one day be pertinent to a possible release through commutation

I did find that all the participants were very thoughtful and fully aware of the likelihood of dying in prison. The most prominent factor that either caused or reinforced a positive adaptation was the death of family members and loved ones. Other research has found that men in similar conditions demonstrated substantial reductions in violations and had no occurrences of hostility as time passed. They remained resilient in their pursuits and held onto hope. They acknowledged that hope is crucial, although clearly it is no easy undertaking (Flanagan, 1981). Maruna (2004) aptly called this "making good." My participants had avoided trouble for decades, demonstrating persistence and deep faith that their behavior may one day lead to a possible release through commutation.

None of the participants pointed out any specific hook that led them to adaptation. Instead, the results suggest it is a combination of factors that leads to adaptation. The factors of time, education, religion, family issues, and psychological adjustment all play a role. The death of family members and loved ones was the most prominent factor to cause or reinforce positive adaptations but was not identified as a hook. This study presented common themes in the men's accounts, demonstrating from inmates' perspective positive adaptation, adjustment, finding new meaning in life, and most importantly, the hope for release and the ability to achieve a second chance.

The results of this study indicated that these men, despite all the hardships they endured, have never relinquished the hope that their rehabilitation will be accepted and recognized, and that they will one day be freed. They never abandon hope and hope intensely molds their behavior. The interviews demonstrated that these men continued to be resilient and to make every effort to adjust and adapt, so as to make themselves good candidates for commutation and parole after decades of incarceration. These behaviors became evident by examining these inmates' newfound attitudes and achievements: they avoided troublesome behavior and took advantage of every available opportunity for education and self-improvement.

CHAPTER 5

Discussion, Conclusions, and Recommendations

This study had a meaningful purpose. It was designed to provide insight into the positive psychological and social effects of adaptive processes. The primary objective was to understand the actual inmates' perspectives and experiences regarding adaptation and adjustment as they experienced it during their life sentence of incarceration. This study found common themes from the men's accounts, revealing positive adaptation, adjustment, and finding new meaning in life. Most importantly, there was a theme of hope for release and the ability to achieve a second chance.

The men in this study, despite all the hardships they have endured, have never relinquished the hope that their rehabilitation will be accepted and recognized, and they will one day be freed. They have never abandoned hope and hope strongly influences their behavior. They continue to be resilient and to make every effort to adjust and adapt to make themselves desirable for commutation and parole, even after decades of incarceration. The inmates' newfound behavior and achievements align with their goal, as they avoided troublesome behavior, and took advantage of every available opportunity for education and self-improvement.

Interpretation of the Findings

Research has not adequately documented the social, psychological, and behavioral changes among older men with life sentences that occur throughout their imprisonment, nor their lived experiences with adjustment and adaptation (Sliva, 2015). My study has begun telling that story. These participants are men who have lived in the hope of one day being heard and understood. As they told their stories they demonstrated their rehabilitation and transition to persons who can safely and productively return to society. They desire to not only make amends for their past, but also make substantial contributions to society.

The peer-reviewed literature documented in Chapter 2 showed the need for additional research and study. Most existing studies are quantitative, outdated, and conducted in Europe rather than America. They present snapshots of prisoner statistics and answer varied academic research questions. None of the extant literature delves into the main issue required to affect positive social change. Smoyer et al. (2019) reported that the research on how those serving sentences achieve positive adjustment and adaptation during incarceration is minimal. Their study emphasized that applying knowledge of inmate adjustment to prison practices is a viable way to improve prisons' efficiency. The present study thus expands our knowledge in an area of sparse research and confirms the need for future studies.

Many aspects of prison adjustment have been identified (Smoyer et al., 2019). Yet the results of these studies have been inconsistent, and many predictors and outcomes are still understudied. For example, the conclusions from two separate studies would leave the reader confused, not knowing who to believe. Johnson and Tabriz (2011) suggested that individuals serving life sentences, with rare exceptions, are a class of living dead. They portray them as sentenced to lonely and untimely deaths due to traumatic stress and anxiety while incarcerated. However, Zamble (1992), who studied lifers for seven years, found that they did not exhibit the traits described by Johnson and Tabriz (2011). The results of this study yielded conclusions that are diametrically opposite to Johnson and Tabriz's. The participants had not shown negative adaptation in ways that would inhibit or make it more challenging to cope. They also did not sink into despair or rebellion. On the contrary, they improved their emotional states, health, and conduct as well as their ability to cope with adversities.

The results of my research confirm Leigey's (2015) conclusion that learning more about how older male prisoners serving life sentences adjust to and cope with prison life is essential to understanding how programs to enhance their ability to adapt can be implemented. Goncalves (2014) described three areas in which prisoners need special help with adjustment. These correctional practices include explaining institutional infractions, healthcare utilization, and coping strategies (Goncalves, 2014). Most extant literature relied on stakeholder groups' perspectives rather than prisoners' perspectives, raising questions of validity. Smoyer et al. (2019) also reported that there were only two qualitative research studies that were peer-reviewed, and they are decades-old. They suggested it was necessary to analyze and utilize existing literature to develop a theoretical framework. This study relied on peer-reviewed literature no more than five years old and utilized older literature only for historical veracity. Bonfield et al. (2018), stated that it is essential to ensure articles are peer-reviewed, relevant to the problem studied, have a purpose, and are focused on the theoretical concept of the study. They also state that, most importantly, the studies need to address a knowledge gap. Miszewski (2017) noted that many earlier studies overlook inmates' positive perspectives or ignored their perspectives in favor of stakeholder views. Overall, there was a focus on and prioritization of the negative aspects.

Based on direct quotes from the participants, I noted the acceptance of the ongoing public narrative stated in colloquial terms, "do the crime, do the time," "adult time for an adult crime," and "tough on crime." These trite phrases contribute to ripping away prisoner's sense of efficacy. Nonetheless, these men have reached a state of acceptance.

As noted in the Introduction, Clemmer (1940) introduced adaptation as an important theory. He stated that prisonization thwarts attempts to rehabilitate inmates and instead inspires behavior contrary to accepted standards of conduct. My results indicated the shortcomings and what I would call the "hasty generalizations" made by Clemmer. Times have changed and so have the long-term inmates. Nelson (1984) built on Clemmer's work and promoted adaptation-level theory. Nelson reported that the earlier studies focused on a specific catalyst for change and merely discussed its value as a catalyst. The early studies seem to overlook the extremely complicated question of "how" adaptation is achieved and the "how" of the adjustment to positive social change. The status of adaptation and adjustment in this study yielded key findings that illustrate the several combinations of factors involved in obtaining positive social adaptation.

Clemmer and Nelson each worked with one or sometimes two themes, avoiding the complication of a multithemed theory. For example, my results show that the various categories are common to more than one participant and are intertwined in evoking positive reactions from the participants.

Each participant was presented with identical questions in the same order. The responses were coded by described phrases and words. The hand-coding was very difficult as it was challenging to understand what was written and the meaning of the emerging patterns/themes. Various categories which developed into subthemes emerged. The findings indicated that no one particular theme was the sole cause or catalyst that led to adaptation. Rather, it was the combinations of the themes acting together which produced this adjustment to the environment of life in prison. The tone of the responses indicated that handling fear and survival were prominent factors leading to resilience. Again, no one theme was named by the participants as being responsible for the adaptation. Interview question 4 evoked a unanimous response from all participants: they hope for release and to become a new man leading a new life.

Nelson (1984) and Crewe et al. (2017) both state that inmates have the ability to adjust to new experiences and information, and that the frameworks for making sense of adaptation and adjustment to prison need to be sociological or psychological. The participants all accepted their wrongdoing. I found that, like any other humans, these men want to put the past behind them and move forward with positive changes. They want to bring meaning to their lives. And the meaning they sought was to prove they could and did become better people. They wanted to prove they earned freedom through merit, and that they can, and one day will, reconcile with society. However, they live in a maximum-security prison where survival is a major concern and isolation is a key survival technique. These inmates were what are called "easy keepers" who caused little or no disruption, follow the rules, and keep to themselves. These behaviors are a successful survival technique. A record of the good behavior was a mandatory requirement to be accepted as a participant in the study. These inmates are given low priority by the correctional staff. They are blocked from access to meaningful education and real job training and have little assistance or opportunities to add meaning to their lives.

The approach of this study allowed for the exploration of every possible variable and for finding its impact. Previous literature omitted or under-represented the inmates' survival mechanisms and the reality of the daily fear they experienced. I found all participants' initial reaction to incarceration was extreme fear and trauma. They turned toward isolation as a way to enhance their survival potential. However, neither fear nor trauma can be claimed as the catalyst to change. My research indicated that time and/or aging was vital in the adaptation process. In other words, the adjustment began slowly and fed on itself. As the men learned more skills, they gained more confidence in themselves and attained additional skills. All my participants achieved their high school educations via a GED program early on in their sentences. While learning to read and write, they gained verbal skills and emotional security. As shown by Flanagan (1981), as the men aged and participated in programs, there were substantial reductions in violations and reduced occurrences of hostility. They remained resilient in their pursuit of their goals and held onto hope. To them, hope is crucial, despite a seemingly hopeless situation. Maruna (2004) called these changes "making good." The inmates in this study made good and continued doing so for decades by avoiding bad behavior. They demonstrated persistence, deep faith, and belief that their behavior would one day lead to a possible release through commutation.

None of the participants revealed any one specific hook that led them to adaptation. My results suggest that there is a necessary combination of factors that leads to adaptation, including time, education, religion, family issues, and psychological adjustment. Of course, the environment is crucial, although I found no singular common theme related to environment. Toch (2002) described the transition as follows:

long-term lifers appear to cope maturely with their confinement by establishing a daily routine that allows them to find meaning and purpose in a life that might otherwise seem empty and pointless. Similarly, the establishment of meaning and purpose was evident in the data collected here. Some inmates adjusted in three or four weeks, some over several years. However, their adjustment never ended the hope to survive and the daily fear of being confronted or attacked and killed by other prisoners.

This study also aligns with Flanagan's (1985) observations that the changes that occur while imprisoned are observable but in an unexpectedly positive direction. He suggested that scholars' thinking about the effect of long-term incarceration has come full circle from the earlier research on the deterioration model. Flanagan also noted that while they adapt and adjust, the strategies they use are not easy to deduce and even more difficult to classify. This is a difficult lesson I learned during this dissertation. In addition, I concur with Mackenzie and Goodstein (1985) that long-term confinement's adverse effects have not been satisfactorily demonstrated in any existing empirical research. As Porporino and Zamble (1984) conclude, the literature on the prison experience is deficient in advancing an understanding of adaptation and the changes that occur in the thoughts and behavior of the LWOP.

Miszewski (2017) aptly points out that the literature on LWOPs is in fact decades old and deals mostly with European countries rather than the United States. While people of color are always over-represented in prisons, it is appalling to note that one of five African American prisoners is serving a life sentence (The Sentencing Project, 2020). In summary, while we have demonstrated through their own voices the changes that occur to the long-term inmates in my study, there is no one explanation of how their identity emerges. It is a complicated phenomenon that requires more study.

Theoretical Concept

This study used adaptation theory as the framework for gaining insight into adaptation's practical function, and how it produced positive changes among long-term inmates. I used this theoretical lens to explore the lifers' perspectives and to understand their experiences. Older men with LWOP sentences realize they must change their ways, and engaging factors (like religion, education, and socialization) help facilitate adaptation and adjustment.

Clemmer's (1940) adaptation theory has been used in various fields, including psychology and criminology. Clemmer's research suggested that prisonization thwarts attempts to rehabilitate convicts and inspires behavior contrary to accepted social conduct standards. Adaptation is the result of encountering new or different environmental conditions or demands and is necessary in order to meet basic needs and maintain a good quality of life. In psychology, adaptation is a process by which individuals or groups make necessary or desired changes: cognitive, behavioral, and affective. Taylor (1983) concludes that humans cope with threats in their lives by creating a set of positive concepts or illusions that serve to protect their psychological health. These positively slanted cognitions create space for hope, personal growth, and flexibility.

The results of this study support adjustment and adaptation as necessary mechanisms that lead to behavior change and positive outcomes among long-term inmates. The subthemes found in this study clearly demonstrate that the men adopted hope, achieved growth, and remained flexible and resilient. These adaptations involved changing cognitions in three domains: searching for deeper meaning in the experience, increasing individual control, and restoring positive self-views. The changed cognitions were evident in the responses of the participants.

Limitations of the Study

Due to the qualitative methodology, this study was subject to potential bias as described in both Creswell (2013) and Patton (2015). Due to my role as the researcher and as the primary data analyst, the study results are subjective in interpretation. Due to the small number of participants, there is a limit to the transferability of the results to larger populations. Lastly, it was assumed the participants provided honest responses to the open-ended, semi-structured interview questions. No attempt was made to validate their answers against objective criteria. Another potential limitation of the research procedure was due to the COVID-19 pandemic. It necessitated a change from face-to-face interviews to written correspondence when the Pennsylvania Department of Corrections eliminated all visitation for 18 months. The inability to observe body language and/or facial expressions restricted the analysis to written responses.

Recommendations

Chapter 2 reviewed findings from existing studies concerning adjustment and adaptation. Toch (1992) found that aging and therefore maturing in prison leads to inmates gaining better self-control. Lifers made their sentences their own by choosing personal routines and going along with the institutional program, which, they came to realize, they cannot change. The results of this current study indicate the participants-maintained control over their incarceration by spending much of their time in solitary pursuits. They also became more thoughtful. However, to answer some of the questions, the participants needed to recall feelings and behaviors from at least 20 years ago. It is well-known that memories can change over time, and even become faulty. Because they have had such a long time to reflect on their life in prison, their responses could be less emotional and more thoughtful than if they responded closer in time to their commitment to prison.

The most important aspect of future studies is to understand the positive adjustment and adaptation of long-term inmates and will require quantitative research. The growing science regarding measuring behavior and advances in methodology may enable a researcher to identify significant determinants and subjective behavioral supports. It is hoped that advances in research on adaptation and adjustment will be recognized as vital factors in understanding the prosocial changes long-term inmates often undergo.

Implications

As the system is today, it is difficult to achieve positive social changes with long-term inmates. Individuals must first be willing to change, including the attitudes of the public. When a prisoner changes, it can be like the proverbial tree falling unwitnessed in the forest. Will society hear their pleas, accept the possibility of change, and acknowledge their changes? While the LWOPs adapt and adjust, no results will be publicly evident unless society supports their need to demonstrate their change. Each of the participants expressed their perspectives on their experiences during their long-term incarceration which expands our knowledge on the needed intervention initiative required. Results of this study reveal the long-term inmates' perspectives and how they differ from the stakeholders' perspective. This understanding of the process as described by the participants may lead to more effective intervention programs and professionals aiding in the commutation process of LWOPs.

The results of this study further confirm the need to focus on the LWOP population and their unnecessary hardships in acquiring educational, vocational, and other developmental programs accessible to only younger inmates.

Many of the themes and summaries within this study can be transformed into educational programs for the LWOPs and for the organizations that support the LWOPs. The problem of men left to die has become an ethical and moral issue. Many scholars and academics have described a lack of attention to the problem of the treatment of long-term incarcerated inmates dying-in prison. By implication, it is time to concentrate efforts and to focus on this problem of oversight. The findings of this report demonstrated that positive adaptation occurs. The stakeholders must take the time to recognize these positive changes. These men are capable of contributing to society and could help implement programs educating youth in the neighborhoods about the pitfalls of drugs and crime. Street youths would respect the input and guidance of these men.

Conclusions

The findings of this study reveal that society could be said to have made a Faustian bargain. Faust refers to the legend of Doctor Faustus, a character in German folklore who made a pact with the devil. A Faustian agreement is one in which a person abandons spiritual or moral principles in order to obtain knowledge, wealth or other benefits. In the prison context, life in prison (LWOP) appears more humane or morally acceptable than execution. The LWOP sentence was the result of a compromise between hard-on-crime advocates and anti-execution lobbyists, pro-lifers, and various religious advocates. The findings of this study illustrate the inconvenient truth that life without parole is not in all senses a moral alternative. It is arguably a travesty of justice and a violation of human rights that is not defensible. LWOP is the death penalty "in sheep's clothing." It supplies a "solution" to the immediate issue, but without an understanding of or regard to future cost or consequences.

By reading the comments of the inmates the reader should realize the importance of the inmates' perspectives over those of institutional stakeholders. Will it be possible to change societies' views of life without parole? By hearing the voices of the long-term prisoner, the reader will learn the truth: that life without parole has turned out to possibly be a worse option than the death penalty. LWOP denies any hope of rehabilitation or redemption, and the basic humanity of prisoners.

The message from the participants is that prison is a harrowing experience. However, if undertaken with mature coping skills, it can be constructive time, as indicated by the present study. The participants established the prison as home and realized that to survive they must adapt - because this is all they have. They avoid trouble and, as stated by Johnson (2002), they make the most of the limited opportunities for work and seek out rehabilitative programs and education. The inmates live by the adage "Do your own time." They took control by doing their personal routines as they aged and matured. They also have become more thoughtful as they aged.

According to Zamble and Porporino (1984) the inmates seem to experience an increase in pro-social attitudes as well as improved psychological profiles. This successful adjustment and adaptation seem to feed on themselves. According to Flanagan (1981) adaptation produces more success, more confidence, and more skills. He goes on to state that, over time, lifers gain emotional maturity, significant increases in verbal intelligence, and demonstrate significant reductions in hostility during their stay in prison. He also stated that recidivism rates for these lifers are extremely low and are almost certainly a byproduct of aging in prison as well as the lessons learned while maturely coping in prison over time.

Hope is the hook. The trouble-free behavior and productive records of adjustment compiled by the lifer is the product of hope. They hope to somehow secure their freedom through commutation and as a result, they gain positive attitudes and behavior. Their ability to avoid trouble for decades while incarcerated and the ability to show faith in the fact that their prison good conduct will one day matter in gaining commutation is their hope for the future. This sense of purpose is key. The question nevertheless remains: these men are reborn, they have a strong message and a mission to bring and to guide their lives, but is society willing to listen?

GLOSSARY OF TERMS

Accommodation: When people encounter information that is entirely new or challenges their existing ideas, they achieve accommodation by changing their mental representations to fit the latest information. They form a new schema to accommodate the data and alter their existing mental categories (Crank, 2014).

Adaptation: In psychology, adaptation is a process by which individuals or groups make necessary or desired changes—cognitive, behavioral, and affective—in response to new environmental conditions or demands to meet basic needs, function, and maintain a good quality of life.

Adjustment: The processes of decision-making and value judgments. For this study, the emphasis of adjustment will be on understanding practical methods for handling relationships, using coping devices for inmates, and enhancing the psychological resources for personal change and growth.

Assimilation: This occurs when people take in new ideas and convert them to fit their current views. People possess concepts or schemas that they use to understand the world surrounding them.

Cognitive theories: Cognitive theories of psychology focus on internal states, such as motivation, problem-solving, decision-making, thinking, and attention. Such approaches strive to explain different mental processes, including how the mind processes information.

Coping: Psychological coping mechanisms are commonly referred to as coping strategies or coping skills. The term coping generally refers to adaptive (constructive) coping strategies: strategies that reduce stress. In contrast, other coping strategies may be understood as maladaptive if they increase stress. (https://psychologydictionary.org/coping)

Humanistic theories: Humanistic psychology theories began to grow in popularity during the 1950s. While earlier theories often focused on abnormal behavior and psychological problems, humanist ideas instead emphasized human beings' essential goodness. Some of the significant humanist theorists included Carl Rogers and Abraham Maslow

Institutionalization: The phenomenon that arises from existing within a prison environment with structured days, reduced freedoms, and a complete change of the lifestyle the inmate was previously accustomed to. "Institutionalization refers to the process by which inmates are shaped and transformed by the institutional environments in which they live … it is the shorthand expression for the adverse psychological effects of imprisonment" (Mound, 2017, p. 122).

Life without the possibility of parole (LWOP): Also termed *death by incarceration* (DBI), these acronyms are used interchangeably in this study to describe the experience of life-sentence without the possibility of parole.

Narrative research: A strategy of inquiry in which the researcher studies individuals' lives and asks one or more individuals to provide stories about their experiences. The researcher often retold or restored this information into a narrative chronology (Clandinin & Connelly, 2000).

Prisonization: The process of accepting the culture and social life of prison society. It can be described as a process whereby newly institutionalized offenders accept prison lifestyles and criminal values. Prisonization forms an informal inmate code.

REFERENCES

Aday, R. H. (2003). *Aging prisoners.* Praeger.

Archer, M. S. (2003*). Structure, agency, and the internal conversation.* Cambridge University Press.

Aging Inmate Population Study. (2006). *PsycEXTRA Dataset.* https://doi.org/10.1037/e519682010-001

Appalachian State University, & Johnson, R. (2015). Doing life: A glimpse into the long-term incarceration experience. *Laws, 4*(3), 559-578. https://doi.org/10.3390/laws4030559

Appleton, C. A. (2010). Living a life more ordinary: Lifers' narratives of change. In *Life after life imprisonment* (pp. 136–169). Oxford University Press. https://doi.org/10.1093/acprof:oso/9780199582716.003.0006

Benkova, K., Stoykov, A., Shosheva, V., Vasilev, R., & Georgiev, Y. (2017). Dynamics of personality changes in prisoners as a result of social work with them. *Trakia Journal of Sciences,* 333–338. https://doi.org/10.15547/tjs.2017.04.01

Biographic Narrative Interpretive Method (BNIM). *The SAGE Encyclopedia of Social Science Research Methods.* https://doi.org/10.4135/9781412950589.n66

Bond, G. D., Thompson, L. A., & Malloy, D. M. (2005). Lifespan differences in the social networks of prison inmates. *The International Journal of Aging and Human Development, 61*(3), 161–178. https://doi.org/10.2190/7h5p-2ahj-l34q-gw9u

Caceral, K. C. (2004). *Prison, Inc.: A convict exposes life inside a private prison.* NYU Press.

Carson, E. A. (2016). *Prisoners in 2013* (NCJ No. 247282). Bureau of Justice Statistics. https://bjs.ojp.gov/content/pub/pdf/p13.pdf

Carson, E. A., & Sabol W. J. (2016). *Prisoners in 2011* (NCJ No. 239808). U.S. Department of Justice, Office of Justice Programs, Bureau of Justice Statistics. https://bjs.ojp.gov/content/pub/pdf/p11.pdf

Clemmer, D. (1940). *The prison community.* Holt, Rinehart & Winston.

Clemmer, D. (1958). *The prison community* (2nd ed.). Holt, Rineharty & Winston.

Cornelius, C. V. M., Lynch, C. J., & Gore, R. (2017). *Aging out of crime: Exploring the relationship between age and crime with agent-based modeling.* Virginia Modeling, Analysis, and Simulation Center.

Crank, B. R. (2010). *Adapting to Incarceration: Inmate Perceptions of Prison Life and Adjustment* [Doctoral dissertation, Georgia State University]. Scholar Works @ Georgia State University. https://scholarworks.gsu.edu/cj_theses/10/

Creswell, J. W., & Creswell, J. D. (2018). *Research design: Qualitative, quantitative & mixed methods approach.* SAGE.

Crewe, B., Hulley, S., & Wright, S. (2017a). The gendered pains of life imprisonment. *The British Journal of Criminology, 57*(6), 1359–1378. https://doi.org/10.1093/bjc/azw088

Crewe, B., Hulley, S., & Wright, S. (2017b). Swimming with the tide: Adapting to long-term imprisonment. *Justice Quarterly, 34*(3), 517-541. https://doi.org/10.1080/07418825.2016.1190394

Crewe, B., Hulley, S., & Wright, S. (2020). *Experiencing long-term imprisonment from young adulthood: Identity, adaptation, and penal legitimacy*. Ministry of Justice Analytical Series, HM Prison & Probation Service.

Dhami, M. K., Ayton, P., & Loewenstein, G. (2007). Adaptation to imprisonment: Indigenous or imported? *Criminal Justice and Behavior, 34*(8), 1085-1100. https://doi.org/10.1177/0093854807302002

Di Lorito, C., Vollm, B., & Dening T. (2018). The individual experience of aging prisoners: Systematic review and meta-synthesis through a good lives model framework: Systematic review on aging prisoners. *International Journal of Geriatric Psychiatry, 33*(2), 252–262. https://doi.org/10.1002/gps.4762

Flanagan, T. J. (1980). Time served and institutional misconduct: Patterns of involvement in disciplinary infractions among long-term inmates. *Journal of Criminal Justice, 8*(6), 357–367. https://doi.org/10.1016/0047-2352(80)90111-7

Flanagan, T. J. (1981). Dealing with long term confinement: Adaptive strategies and perspectives among long-term prisoners. *Criminal Justice and Behavior, 8*(2), 201–222. https://doi.org/10.1177%2F009385488100800206

Flanagan, T. J. (1982a). Correctional policy and the long-term prisoner. *Crime and Delinquency, 28*(1), 82–95. https://doi.org/10.1177/001112878202800106

Flanagan, T. J. (1982b). Lifers and long-termers: Doing big time. In R. Johnson & H. Toch (Eds.), *The Pains of Imprisonment* (pp. 115–128). Waveland Press.

Flanagan, T. J. (1995). Adaptation and adjustment among long-term prisoners. In *Long-term imprisonment: Policy, science, and correctional practice* (pp. 109-116). Sage.

Flatt, J. D., Williams, B. A., Barnes, D., Goldenson, J., & Ahalt, C. (2017). Post-traumatic stress disorder symptoms and associated health and social vulnerabilities in older jail inmates. *Aging & Mental Health, 21*(10), 1106-1112. https://doi.org/10.1080/13607863.2016.1201042

Glense, C. (2016). *Becoming qualitative researchers: An introduction* (5th Ed.). Pearson.

Graham, H., & McNeill, F. (2017). Desistance: Envisioning futures. In P. Carlen & L. A. Franca (Eds.), *Alternative Criminologies* (pp. 433–451). Routledge.

Goffman, E. (1961). On the characteristics of total institutions. In *Symposium on preventive and social psychiatry* (pp. 43–84). Walter Reed Army Medical Center.

Gottschalk, M. (2014). *Caught: The prison state and the lockdown of American politics*. Princeton University Press.

Haugebrook, S., Zgoba, K. M., Maschi, T., Morgen, K., & Brown, D. (2010). Trauma, stress, health, and mental health issues among ethnically diverse older adult prisoners. *Journal of Correctional Health Care, 16*(3). 220-229. https://doi.org/10.1177/1078345810367482

Hayes, A. J. (2017). Aging inside: Older adults in prison. In B. Elger, C. Ritter, & H. Stöver (Eds.), *Emerging Issues in Prison Health*. Springer. https://doi.org/10.1007/978-94-017-7558-8_1

Henry, J. S. (2012). Death in prison sentences: Overutilized and underscrutinized. In C. J. Ogletree, Jr., & A. Sarat (Eds.), *Life without parole: America's new death penalty?* (pp. 66–95). New York University Press.

Herbert, S. K. (2017). Inside or outside? Expanding the narratives about life-sentenced prisoners. *Punishment & Society, 20*(5), 628–645. https://doi.org/10.1177/1462474517737048

Herbert, S. K. (2019). *Too easy to keep: Life-sentenced prisoners and the future of mass incarceration*. University of California Press.

Irwin, J. (1997). *It's about time: American's imprisonment binge* (2nd ed.). Wadsworth.

Jarrett, B. (2018). How prison changes people. *Reframing justice*, https://www.reframingjustice.com

Johnson, R., & McGunigall-Smith, S. (2008). Life without parole, America's other death penalty: Notes on life under a death sentence by incarceration. *The Prison Journal, 88*(2), 328-346.

Johnson, R., & Toch, H. (Eds.). (1982) *The pains of imprisonment*. Sage. (Google Scholar)

Johnson, R., & Dobrzanska. A. (2005). Mature coping among life-sentenced inmates: An exploratory study of adjustment dynamics. *Corrections Compendium, 8-9*, 36-38.

Kazemian, L. (2020a). *Can people change for the better in prison?* Retrieved from https://thecrimereport. org/2020/01/16/can-people-change-for-the-better-in-prison/

Kazemian, L. (2020b). *Growth and redemption in prison: finding light behind bars and beyond*. Routledge.

Kazemian, L., & Travis, J. (2015) Imperative for the inclusion of long-termers and lifers in research and policy. *Criminology and Public Policy, 14*(2), 355-395.

Lattimore, P. K., Dawes, D., & Barrick, K. L. (2018). Desistance from crime over the life course: Washington Square Press. Final summary report: Prepared for the National Institute of Justice. RTI International.

Leigey, M. E. (2007). Life while serving life: Examining the correctional experiences of older inmates serving a life without parole sentence. ProQuest. (Microform edition 3277821).447. https://doi. org/10.1177/0093854887014004002

Leigey, M. E. (2015). *The forgotten men: serving a life without parole sentence*. Rutgers University Press.

Leigey, M. E., & Ryder, M. A. (2014). The pains of permanent imprisonment. *International Journal of Offender Therapy and Comparative Criminology, 59*(7), 726–742. https://doi.org/10.1177/0306624x13517868

Maschi, T., and Aday, R. (2014). The social determinants of health and justice and the gaining in prison crisis: A call for human rights action. *International Journal of Social Work, 1*(1), 15-33.

Maschi, T. M., & Morgen, K. (2014). Trauma and stress, coping resources, and mental well-being among older adults in prison. *PsycEXTRA Dataset*, 188–200. https://doi.org/10.1037/e543422014-001

Mauer & Nellis (2018). *The meaning of life: The case for abolishing life sentences*. The New Press.

Meijers, J., Harte, J. M., Jonker, F. A., & Meynen, G. (2017). Prison brain? Executive dysfunction in prisoners. *Frontiers in Psychology, 6*, 43. doi: 10.3389/fpsyg.2015.0004

Miller, R. (2018). *Life without parole in Pennsylvania*. Decarcerate, PA.

Miszewski, K. (2017). *Adaptation to prison isolation of long-term prisoners in Poland: 'Good' and 'bad' adaptation in the light of the adaptation typology of Erving Goffman* (Working paper). https://www. researchgate.net/publication/320531716

Mound, K. (2017). *The long-term effects of incarceration on inmates*. Entity. https://www.entitymag.com/ effects-of-incarceration-inmates/

Nellis, A. (2013). *Life goes on: The historic rise in life sentences in America*. The Sentencing Project.

Nellis, A. (2017). Still life: America's increasing use of life and long-term sentences. Retrieved from www. sentencingproject.org/doc/doc/publications

Paternoster, R., Bachman, R., Kerrison, E., O'Connell, D., & Smith, L. (2016). Desistance from crime and identity. *Criminal Justice and Behavior, 43*(9), 1204-1224. https://doi.org/10.1177/0093854816651905

Paulich, J. (2004). *A life for a life: Life imprisonment: America's other death penalty*. Roxbury Publishing Co.

Prison Policy Initiative. (2019). *Mass Incarceration: The Whole Pie 2020*. https://www.prisonpolicy.org/ reports/pie2020.html

Ravitch, S. M. & Carl, N. M. (2016). *Qualitative research: Bridging the conceptual, theoretical, and methodological*. Sage Publications.

Rogers, K. M., Corley, K. G., & Ashforth, B. E. (2017). (rep.). *Seeing More than Orange: Organizational Respect and Positive Identity Transformation in a Prison Context* (2nd ed., Vol. 62, pp. 219–269). Sage Publications.

Sentencing Project. (2020). *The sentencing project releases its 2019 annual report.* https://www.sentencingproject.org/publications/8008/

Shover, N. (1985). The late stages of ordinary property offender careers. *Social Problems, 31*(2), 208-218.

Singer, M. (2011). Human behavior in the prison environment adaptation as survival. In *Silberman voices* (Vol. 6, pp. 1–17).

Sliva, S. M. (2015). On the meaning of life: A qualitative interpretive meta-synthesis of the lived experience of life without parole. *Journal of Social Work, 15*(5), 498-515. https://www.doi.org/10.1177/1468017314550748

Smith, R. (2015, September 28). Humane criminal justice is not hopeless. https://state.com/news-and-politics/2015/09/pope-francis-and-supreme-court-on0cruel-and-unusual-punishment--dath-penalty-life-without-parole

Smoyer, A. B., Elumn Madera, J., & Blankenship, K. M. (2019). Older adults' lived experience of incarceration. *Journal of Offender Rehabilitation, 58*(3), 220-239. https://doi.org/10.1080/10509674.2019.1582574

Sorensen, J., and Wrinkle, R. D. (1998). No hope for parole: Disciplinary infractions among death-sentenced and life without-parole inmates. *Criminal Justice and Behavior 23*(4), 542-552. doi: 10.177/0032885598078003002

Sorensen, J. R., & Reidy, T. J. (2018). Nothing to lose? An examination of prison misconduct among life-without-parole inmates. *The Prison Journal, 99*(1), 46–65. https://doi.org/10.1177/0032885518814719

Sparkes, A. C., & Day, J. (2016). Aging bodies and desistance from crime: Insights from the life stories of offenders. *Journal of Aging Studies, 36*, 47–58. https://doi.org/10.1016/j.jaging.2015.12.005

Sykes, G. M. (1958). *The society of captives: A study of a maximum-security prison.* Princeton University Press.

Taylor, A. J. W. (1961). Social isolation and imprisonment. *Psychiatry, 24*, 373-376.

Taylor, C. F. N. (2011). What is the difference between desistance and resilience? Exploring the relationship between two key concepts. *Youth Justice, 11*(3), 221–234. https://doi.org/10.1177/1473225411420528

Taylor, S. E. (1983). Adjustment to threatening events: A theory of cognitive adaptation. *American Psychologist, 38*(11), 1161–1173. doi:10.1037/0003-066X.38.11.1161

Toch, H. (1975). *Peacekeeping: Police, prisons, and violence.* Lexington Books.

Toch, H. (1992). *Living in prison: The ecology of survival.* American Psychological Association.

Toch, H. (2009). "I am not now who I used to be then": Risk assessment and the maturation of long-term prison inmates. *The Prison Journal, 90*(1), 4–11. https://doi.org/10.1177/0032885509356408

Webster, R. (2017). *Keeping up with drugs and crime.* https://www.russellwebster.com/author/russellwebster

Wormith, J. S. (1984). The controversy over the effects of long-term incarceration. In T. J. Flanagan (Ed.), *Long-term imprisonment: Policy, science, and correctional practice.* Reprinted from *Canadian Journal of Criminology,* 1984.

Wright, K. N. (1989). Race and economic marginality in explaining prison adjustment. *Journal of Research in Crime and Delinquency, 26*(1), 67–89. https://doi.org/10.1177/0022427889026001004

APPENDIX A: RECRUITMENT FLYER

Narrative of Adjustment and Adaptation among Older Males Serving Life Sentences

A research study and proposal are being conducted by John Taglianetti, a researcher and doctoral candidate at Walden University, Minneapolis, Minnesota. The project is under the direction of Dr. Ethel Perry and Dr. Sharon Xeuerb, members of Walden University faculty. John seeks to recruit 15 older males to meet the requirements for this study who have reached 50 and have served a minimum of 20 years in a maximum-security prison. By conducting narrative interviews with the older male Lifers, we can better understand how the long-term prisoner adjusts and adapts and how this phenomenon and the collected phenomena impact prosocial attitudes and relationships.

You will be considered eligible to participate in this study if you are at least 50 years of age, have served a minimum of 20 consecutive years in a maximum-security prison, are fluent in English, literate and not requiring a legal guardian, not currently mentally or physically ill, have not been suicidal in past 365 days, have not suffered a bipolar or any manic episode in past 30 days, and are willing to consent to audio recorded interviews, whether in person, by Skype, or Zoom formats.

Your participation will be entirely voluntary, and there is no expected direct benefit nor compensation. A series of two written interviews to verify results will be held. The interviews are designed to study your experiences regarding adaptation and adjustment while you are incarcerated. If you are interested in participating in this study, contact John Taglianetti at john.taglianetti@waldenu.edu, or via the GTL connect network within the prison, or my direct phone line 267-626-7051.

APPENDIX B: INFORMED CONSENT

Consent Form

You are invited to participate in a research study and proposal conducted by John Taglianetti, a doctoral researcher at Walden University, Minneapolis, Minnesota. The project is under the direction of Dr. Ethel Perry and Dr. Sharon Xeuerb, members of Walden University faculty. John seeks to recruit 15 older males to meet the requirements for this study who have reached 50 and have served a minimum of 20 years in a maximum-security prison. By conducting narrative interviews with the older male Lifers, we can better understand how the long-term prisoner adjusts and adapts and how this phenomenon and the collected phenomena impact prosocial attitudes and relationships. This form is known as Informed Consent, enabling the participants to understand this study and make an informed decision before participating in the program.

Background Information

The written interviews are designed to explore and divulge the inmates' perspectives on adjustment and adaptation to long-term prison sentences and attempt to understand them better and discover how the prisoner adjusts and adapts and the resulting impact on prosocial development attitudes and relationships.

Procedures

If you decide to participate in this study, you will be asked to do the following:

- Return signed response to the advertisement.
- Return signed copy of Informed Consent.
- Participate in two interviews, each scheduled two weeks apart, and a final interview, scheduled two weeks after the first interview.
- The interviews are confidential, and you will be assigned a code number that is not disclosed to anyone other than the research supervisors at Walden University.

You can also email me or call me if you have questions before, during, or after any interview session. This follow-up communication is voluntary and solely for the participants' ease of communication.

Nature of the Study

This research study is entirely voluntary, and you can accept or reject the invitation without any consequences whatsoever. You can continue the study, leave the study, or change your mind at any time. As all inmates are being contacted, the researcher will follow up with all volunteers to let them know whether they were selected for the study.

Payment

No payment or personal benefit is received by participating in the research project.

Risks and Benefits

This study will not pose any risk to your well-being or physical safety. However, there may be some risk of discomfort, stress, fatigue, or upset due to the subject matter. The benefit could be using the results to improve effective policy for LWOPs and Lifers serving life sentences, leading to a better parole opportunity.

Privacy

The participants' identity is confidential, always protected, and never disclosed, as the researcher will utilize pseudonyms and not disclose the location. Data is stored in secure, password-protected files in the researcher's secure site. No identifiable information will be available, and only the researcher has data access, which will be kept for five years as required by the university. Confidentiality mandates that past crimes will not be reported; however, the potential danger to self or others must be reported.

Contacts

Ask questions either now or later via email, john.taglianetti@waldenu.edu, or by telephone, at 267-626-7051. If you have privacy concerns, you can call the Research Participant Advocate at Walden University, at 612-302-1210.

If you feel you understand this study well enough to make an informed decision, please indicate your consent

If you are doing so by email use, reply to your email with the words, "I consent."

Otherwise, sign and send below

Printed Name of Participant   _____

Date of Consent   _____

Signature of Participant   _____

Signature of Researcher   _____